Saudi Arabian
SEASHELLS

Saudi Arabian
SEASHELLS

Selected Red Sea and Arabian Gulf molluscs

DOREEN SHARABATI

VNU Books International

First published in 1981

© 1981 Doreen Phillips Sharabati

Library of Congress Catalog Card number 81-52534

British Library Cataloguing in Publication Data

Sharabati, Doreen
   Saudi Arabian seashells.
   I. Shells—Saudi Arabia
   I. Title
   594.0953   QL426.S/

ISBN 0-9507641-0-8

Photographs on the title pages, the opposite
page and pages 7, 9 and 10 are in order of
appearance: *Chicoreus ramosus, Lambis truncata
sebae, Fasciolaria trapezium, Conus textile,
Streptopinna saccata, Conus textile—Red Sea
specimens. (Kit Constable-Maxwell)*

Designed by Moira Shippard

Phototypeset in Monophoto Garamond
by MS Filmsetting Ltd, Frome, Somerset

Printed in the Netherlands
by Royal Smeets Offset B. V. Weert

Contents

Acknowledgements

Many people have helped to bring this book to completion. I am grateful to the photographers who provided more and better pictures than I could have produced alone. Special thanks go to my husband and Gunnar Bemert, who provided the bulk of the underwater photography and companionship on many dives. Kit Constable-Maxwell's splendid still-life studies of shells have added an artistic dimension to this book and I am happy to have had his enthusiastic participation in the project since its inception.

This book could not have been completed without the special co-operation and help given me by Dr. John D. Taylor and his staff at the British Museum of Natural History, where I spent many happy hours in the library. Dr. Taylor has also spent many hours proof-reading and making corrections and suggestions and I am greatly indebted to him. I do, however, take full responsibility for any existing errors. Others who read parts of the manuscript and made corrections or suggestions were Dr. Rupert Ormond, Dr. R. Tucker Abbott, Bob Greene, Sir Patrick Skipwith and Mrs. Kathleen Smythe.

Having good specimens to photograph is important and I appreciate the generosity of Brock and Linda Staniland (ARAMCO Environmental Unit), Jackie Gunn, Betty Vincett, Grant Wilson, Ron Williams and Andrew Mollard, for loaning me shells. Reema Safadi Kabbani and Heather Ross graciously donated examples of the uses of shells. Specimens must be identified, and John Shidler, Dr. Taylor, Kathy Way, Solene Morris and Dr. Greg Brown helped in this endeavor.

For consultation on special questions, Waddah Faris and Zakia Bushnak Bakheet were very helpful. In the early stages of the project, Cynthia Fetterolf was most encouraging, as was Heather Ross who, together with her husband Barry, offered me their generous hospitality throughout the project.

This work would never have been completed without the support of The Ministry of Foreign Information for the Kingdom of Saudi Arabia, which urged me to write the book.

My good friend Val Hodges, has spent innumerable hours during the past year helping me with the manuscript-typing and retyping, proof-reading, and serving as my quintessential reader. Kathy Fraser spent many laborious hours editing and indexing, for which I am also grateful.

Above all, I thank my husband, Issam, who taught me to dive and has shared many intriguing hours underwater with me. It was he who first suggested this work and searched the seas, beaches and books throughout the project with me, and to him I dedicate my effort.

Foreword

Saudi Arabia is a unique country blessed with an unusual natural history. In addition to its fascinating land fauna and flora, Saudi Arabia can boast of marine waters rich in sealife.

Seashells are part of the environmental riches of this country, and both shores of the Arabian Peninsula—the Red Sea and the Gulf—have their unique assemblage of molluscs. Doreen Sharabati has championed the cause of protecting the marine beauty of Saudi Arabia, and this delightful book will open a new world of wonder for visitors and local citizens alike. She tells the story of shells, how and where they live and, through beautiful photography, introduces her readers to the inspiring hobby of malacology.

R. Tucker Abbott Ph.D.
President
American Malacologists, Inc.
Melbourne, Florida, U.S.A.

Preface

At the time of writing there is no book in print about the seashells of the Red Sea or those of the Arabian Gulf. Because these bodies of water are semi–enclosed and fairly well separated from the Indian Ocean, they are inhabited by shells that, in many cases, are unique. The small amount of literature about Red Sea and Gulf shells is primarily of a scientific nature, scattered in professional journals and inappropriate to most general readers. Even available checklists of shells from these regions are of little use or interest to a casual admirer of shells, as they too are intended for scientists. This book will serve as a layman's introduction to shells, especially those that can be found in the coastal waters of Saudi Arabia. Because many of the shells found there range widely throughout the Indo-Pacific, this book can also be of value to collectors interested in the entire region.

It is difficult to organize and represent in a first book all of the thousands of shells found in a single area. Some live only in very deep waters and are rarely seen. Others are not numerous or are so minute that a microscope is needed to see them, and a scientist might have trouble identifying them even after dissecting the soft-bodied animals that live inside. Of the seven classes of animal making up the phylum Mollusca, only the three most likely to be encountered in the Red Sea and Gulf regions will be represented photographically in this volume. Typical examples of the more common orders of mollusc will be included to assist the interested reader in making identifications. A systematic classification of shells will not, however, be attempted, although a reference book of this type is currently being compiled.

Although it is customary in scientific works on molluscs to include, as part of the scientific name, the surname of the authority originally naming a species, this volume will list complete names in the index only. The book is not intended as a complete identification manual or guide for shell collectors, although every effort has been made to ensure that the information included is scientifically correct. Rather, this book is intended as an introduction to the enchanting world of seashells, the fascinating lives that they lead, the wonder of their abilities, and the beauty of their structures. The photographer Feininger has found it amazing that ". . . an apparently insignificant lump of slime can produce permanent housings of often breathtaking beauty, daring, originality, exquisite color, and superlative geometric perfection. . . ." The artist in the author has tried to focus on the aesthetic quality of these creatures, while the educator in her has attempted to convey enough information to satisfy the curiosity of the general reader who wants information as much as aesthetic visual stimulation. Although it is their fantastic beauty and variety that initially attract attention, seashells cannot be fully appreciated without an understanding of the way the animals inhabiting them live, because their needs, environment, and evolutional development determine the external appearance of their shells. This book, therefore, includes sections explaining how the bodies of these animals are structured, where they live, and how they manage to live there.

The sea is a fairly stable environment, but even the slightest change in a single factor can destroy that stability. Present technology is not sufficiently advanced to allow marine molluscs to live in aquariums exactly as they would in the sea. It is, therefore, easier to show the beauty of these living animals by photographing them in their natural habitat rather than by displaying them in an artificial environment. Photographs collected in a book have several advantages—they can be seen by more people than could ever visit a particular aquarium, and they can be enjoyed at leisure and referred to time and again for information and pleasure. For these reasons, this book contains many photographs of live marine molluscs in their underwater habitats. Where it has proved impossible to obtain photographs of live molluscs, it has been attempted, as far as practicable, to portray the shells in settings that would at least inspire a sense of their natural habitats.

These beautiful animals also serve to introduce people to the natural history of the Kingdom of Saudi Arabia by conveying an idea of the unique environment of the Red Sea and Arabian Gulf. If people can learn to appreciate the fragility of these waters, perhaps they will support efforts to conserve them. As the world's attention is increasingly focused on the environment, its natural inhabitants, and their fight for survival, the author hopes that this contribution will help to raise the general level of interest in natural history. If this objective has been achieved to any degree, the effort will have been worthwhile.

A note on conservation

Most of the changes affecting the sea are natural in origin. Continental drift and climatic fluctuations, such as ice ages and the resultant alterations in mean sea temperature and levels, often took thousands of years to manifest themselves, whereas earthquakes or volcanic eruptions can change things abruptly and effectively; for example, fine volcanic ash can suffocate molluscan larva. Seasonal climatic changes are, of course, also an important factor in determining which species are present in a given area, for an especially low spring tide or an unusually heavy frost can affect the population catastrophically.

Although major alterations in the marine environment are usually natural, man also affects the sea. Manmade changes most often result from uncontrolled development due to population growth, exploitation of natural resources, shipping, or industrial installations. Industrial facilities are often situated on a coast to be near water for cooling purposes and docking facilities. The building of docks alters the movement of marine sediments and often causes a change in, or a loss of, some of the molluscan community. If the seawater used for cooling comes from restricted localities, (that is, inside a fringing reef), its reintroduction can lead to a rise in the mean sea temperature, a form of thermal pollution causing an increased growth of flora and fauna, and the oxygen-carrying capacity of the water will be reduced. These and other altered conditions may lead to the establishment of aggressive exotic species and possibly other, as yet unknown changes.

In the process of loading and discharging cargoes between docks and ships, there is nearly always some loss. If crude oil is the cargo, the lighter, more volatile, fractions can cause even more damage than the heavier fractions, which become less toxic when they are exposed to air and are, in fact, biodegradable. Damage can occur just as easily from the efforts to clean up after oil spills because these operations often use detergents that are toxic to intertidal molluscs (especially disastrous if these molluscs happen to be commercially valuable, edible bivalves).

Other types of problem are associated with urbanization. As development progresses, beaches quickly become depleted of indigenous communities of flora and fauna because commercial developers require flat, well-drained building land. Use of the seashore for recreation and tourism, if it is uncontrolled, will also result in degeneration. Another manmade danger is contamination by pesticides and chemicals, although, in fact, these are often more harmful to humans and animals than they are to the molluscs inhabiting an area, as the molluscs can accumulate bioconcentrations of pollutants that may toxically affect the animal (man) eating them without being harmed themselves. This is less of a threat in the Red Sea, however, for no rivers draining agricultural lands flow into it. The problem arises especially with bivalves collected near domestic waste outlets, which often discharge directly into the fringing lagoons in front of areas of strip development.

The fishing industry has been aware of the benefits of marine conservation for many years, and they have recently been joined by the fish farmers. The marine farming approach should be encouraged, but, if it is to succeed, coastal waters must be kept clean. The coral reef system depends on the efficient recycling of nutrients, and the removal or alteration of more than a limited proportion of any one factor could result in a breakdown of the entire system.

The coral reefs of the Red Sea are in better condition than many located elsewhere because industrial pollution and commercial activities are still localized, but, as development increases, they could be significantly affected. Although the need for marine conservation is not quite as urgent in the Red Sea as it is in other places, it is essential to enact conservation measures now while the vested interests in the sparsely developed stretches of coastline are still few. It is indicative that the beginnings of coral reef deterioration are at present most marked near the head of the Gulf of Aqaba and in the immediate vicinity of Jeddah, where there has been considerable pressure to utilize the available coastline.

Saudi Arabia began to consider marine conservation measures in the last decade when the countries bordering the Red Sea, under the auspices of the Arab League Educational, Scientific and Cultural Organization (ALESCO) and the UN Environmental Program (UNEP), began developing a regional marine environmental program. In connection with this project, the International Union for the Conservation of Nature (IUCN) has been developing a program related to critical marine habitats. One of the IUCN's efforts has been the establishment of a network of marine reserves throughout the region.

The marine conservation policy drawn up for the Red Sea requires legislation and action to prevent widespread pollution (especially important in this semi-enclosed sea). Selection and protection of sites containing representative samples of habitats and species, protection throughout the area of particular species, (for example, dugongs, turtles, manta rays, and whale sharks), and encouragement of measures to minimize the degradation of marine environments throughout the area are urgent necessities.

In 1978, the countries bordering the Gulf joined together to launch the Kuwait Action Plan for the Protection and Development of the Marine Environment and Coastal Areas. By 1981, an environmental assessment and management survey of the region had been undertaken and operational documents drawn up. A regional trust fund was established and the grounds for the establishment of the Marine Emergencies Mutual Aid center were prepared. The UN Environments Program supervised the implementation of the KAP and will continue, with other UN organizations, to serve as advisers to the regional governments in their cooperative efforts to protect and develop the Gulf region.

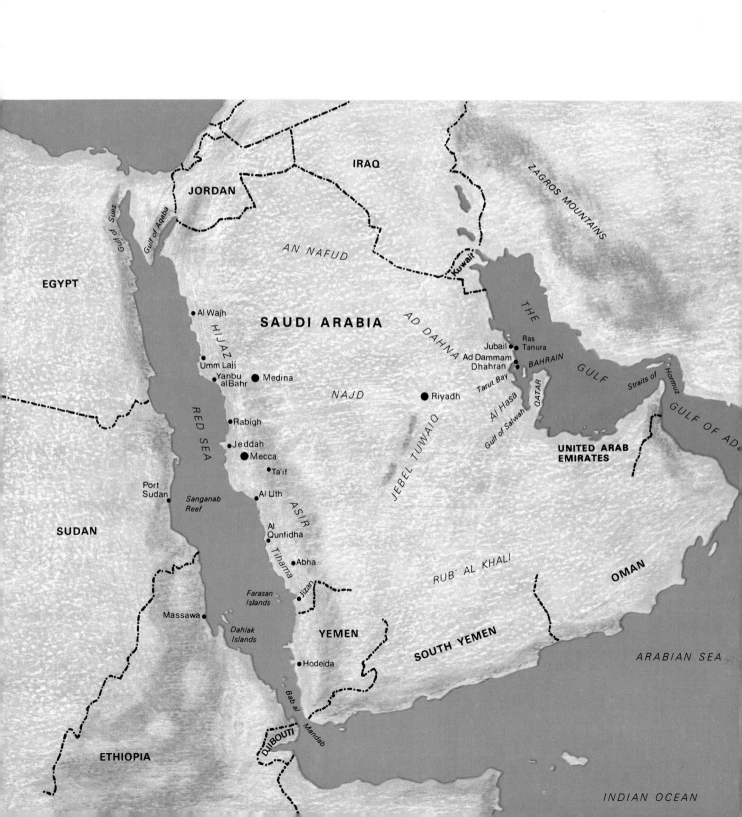

1 The geography of the area

Saudi Arabia

The Arabian Peninsula lies on a northwest–southeast axis between the Red Sea and the Arabian Gulf. It is largely a huge plateau that geologic movements caused to tilt slightly to the east. Its western and southern edges moved upward at the same time as these movements and created a valley that became the Red Sea. In the western part of the country, the almost flat plateau of old crystalline rock extends to an impressive mountain escarpment, which parallels the Red Sea coast from the Gulf of Aqaba in the north to the Gulf of Aden in the south. This escarpment is divided in the vicinity of Mecca. In the northern half, called the Hijaz, the mountains reach 2,100 meters and decrease to 610 meters in the area of the gap near Mecca. The more rugged mountains south of Mecca are called the Asir and have peaks that reach 3,050 meters. In the south, a coastal plain, the Tihama lowlands, rises gradually from the sea to the mountains.

From the western escarpment, the plateau slopes gently down to the east, interrupted by the Tuwaiq Mountains, a lower range that curves in a westward crescent from the north to the south through Riyadh. To the east of these mountains, the slope is even more gentle, and the land is nearly flat all the way to the coast of the Gulf.

The Kingdom of Saudi Arabia encompasses approximately 80 per cent of the Arabian Peninsula and totals over 2,240,000 square kilometers. The entire western boundary of the Kingdom is the Red Sea; the two Yemens edge the southern borders. To the north lie Jordan, Iraq, and Kuwait; to the east are the Arabian Gulf, the island of Bahrain, the peninsula of Qatar, the United Arab Emirates, and the Sultanate of Oman.

The Kingdom has six natural geographic regions—the Hijaz, the Asir, the Najd, the northern region, the eastern region and the Rub'al Khali.

The northern half of the region of the Red Sea escarpment is called the Hijaz. This area contains the busy port city of Jeddah, which is the business center of the Kingdom. Jeddah is also the gateway for the more than a million Moslem pilgrims a year who come through the Islamic Port on pilgrimage to the two holiest cities of Islam—Mecca, site of Islam's most sacred shrine, the Ka'aba, and Medina, the burial place of the Prophet Mohammad. Another seaport 400 kilometers north of Jeddah, Yanbu' al Bahr, is now being made into a new industrial city complex and will be connected by oil and gas pipelines to Jubail, a similar industrial city complex being constructed on the east coast. Ta'if, which lies at a height of about 1,600 meters in the mountains almost due east of Jeddah, is also in the Hijaz. In the hot season, when temperatures in

Riyadh soar to more than 49°C, the Saudi Government moves to Ta'if, the traditional summer capital.

South of Mecca to the border of Yemen is the Asir region, which also borders the Red Sea. A salty tidal plain runs along the coast, but, further inland, the land has rich potential. The slopes are well watered and extensively terraced higher in the mountains, and some receive an average of 35 centimeters of rain per year, which is enough to permit non-irrigated cultivation. The highest parts of the Asir have the only areas of natural forest in the country. Several fertile wadis (intermittently flowing stream beds) are found in the plateau region that slopes eastward from the mountains. The weather in the Asir is often frosty and drops below freezing at night in the winter.

The vast, high plateau at the heart of Saudi Arabia is called the Najd. At the center of this region lies the capital city of Riyadh. One of the two largest cities in the Kingdom, it has, like Jeddah, reached nearly a million inhabitants. This area of the Peninsula's plateau slopes from an elevation of about 1,350 meters in the west to about 750 meters in the east, a short distance beyond the Tuwaiq Mountain range, which itself rises 120 to 240 meters above the plateau. Many fingerlike wadis are eroding into this plateau of gently dipping sedimentary rocks. A long strip of sand desert, the Dahna, only about 48 kilometers wide separates the Najd from the eastern region. This desert, sometimes called the "river of sand", is the smallest of the three deserts in the Kingdom and extends from the Nafud in the north to the Rub' al Khali in the south. Along its edges are extensive pans of fine silt, which, in the rainy season, are flooded to a depth of several centimeters; the resulting temporary lakes may last two to three months. The carpets of annuals and other plants that soon surround these lakes give the area its other name, *raudha* (valley of flowers in Arabic); the plural of this word, *riyadh*, gave the capital its name. Although there are some oases in its northern part, the Najd is mostly arid and averages less than 10 centimeters of rain per year. When it rains occasionally in summer, it is so hot that sometimes the raindrops evaporate while they fall or as soon as they touch the hot ground. It can also be several years between rainfalls.

The northern region lies in the angle between the borders of Jordan and Iraq. It contains the second largest sand desert in the Kingdom, the Nafud, which features reddish dunes up to 100 meters high and many kilometers long and separated by valleys as much as 16 kilometers wide. North of the Nafud is an upland plateau covered with grass and scrub steppe vegetation used for pasture by the bedouin. Also remarkable in this region is the large Wadi Sirhan basin remaining from an ancient inland sea, which is up to 300 meters below the surrounding plateau.

The eastern region, once called Al Hasa after the murmuring waters of the Kingdom's largest oasis, is of great agricultural potential. The richest of all the regions, it contains the largest petroleum fields in the world. The headquarters of the Arabian-American Oil Company (ARAMCO) are located in Dhahran, a few miles from the provincial administrative capital and port of Dammam. North of Dhahran is Ras Tanura, the world's largest petroleum port, and still further north is Jubail, the site of one of the Kingdom's two new industrial complexes.

The Gulf coastal plain, about 160 kilometers in width, merges almost indefinably with the coast and sea in an unstable mixture of salt flats, shoals and reefs, marshes, and sandy plain. Severe sand and dust storms called *shammals* that can blow almost continuously from the northwest in the late spring and early summer reduce visibility to a few feet.

Along the Gulf coast, as along the Red Sea, the dry desert climate gives way to humidity that is often between 85 and 100 per cent.

The region called the Rub' al Khali, or the Empty Quarter, is the largest continuous body of sand in the world. It covers an area of 650,000 square kilometers and has several different types of dunes. The soft sand, in longitudinal and crescent-shaped dunes, is found in the west where the elevation is about 610 meters. Farther east at lower altitudes, the surface is often covered by salt flats and sand sheets. Occasionally, there are long sand dunes and, rarely, sand mountains up to 300 meters in height. Although it seems devoid of life to the casual observer, this desert as "recently" as 10,000 years ago teemed with gazelle, antelope, lion, hippopotamus, and other animals now associated with African savannahs.

Although there are no lakes and almost no permanent streams in Saudi Arabia, wadis abound. Otherwise, sweet water is to be found only in scattered oases, where some meager agriculture is pursued by drawing

A sandy beach by the Red Sea.
(*Gunnar Bemert*)

17

water from springs and wells. Recently, public and private desalination plants have begun to produce large amounts of water for drinking, agriculture, new industries, and construction; a pleasant by-product of these facilities is the gardens and flowers that are making cities such as Jeddah newly green.

The Red Sea

Extending approximately 1,900 kilometers in a northwest–southeast direction, the Red Sea is a lush oasis of coral life surrounded by vast tracts of desolate mountain and plain. On the African side it is bordered by Egypt, Sudan, Ethiopia, and Djibouti. Along the Arabian coast, the Red Sea washes the arid shores of Saudi Arabia, Yemen, and South Yemen. In all of this coastline, there is no permanent river flowing into the Red Sea and the northern half has very little rainfall. The Red Sea splits in the north into the shallow Gulf of Suez and the deeper Gulf of Aqaba. At its southern end, it narrows to the Straits of Bab al Mandab, the "Gate of Tears", where it joins the Indian Ocean via the Gulf of Aden.

Evidence of previous changes in sea level can be seen in the small cliffs or banks lying from a few meters to a few hundred meters inland and rising abruptly to heights of 5 to 20 meters above the present sea level. Examination of the front edges of these cliffs shows numerous old skeletons of coral intermixed with very worn and semi-fossilized shells and the remains of other marine organisms; these skeletons are the relics of extensive fringing reefs present during a higher sea level about 80,000 years ago. From the Saudi town of Al Wajh in the north to Yemen in the south, there is an almost continuous band of these old reef terraces intermixed with raised beaches, sand dunes, and occasional beds of gravel. Between these raised former reefs and the coast, a lower belt of supratidal *sabkhah* (crusted areas overlying wet sediments) is often found inshore of sand bars, chains of islands, mangroves, or quiet lagoons. In addition, scuba divers exploring the fringing reefs commonly find another large step or terrace about 5 meters below sea level and ranging from a few to 50 meters wide, possible evidence of a time when the sea level was lower.

North of Al Wajh, the average width of the coastal plain and shelves combined is less than 2 kilometers; between Al Wajh and Jeddah, the width increases to 15 kilometers; south of Jeddah, the coastal plain widens until it reaches a maximum of about 40 kilometers at Jizan, where the coastal shelf also widens to 100 kilometers and includes the Farasan Islands.

The central channel of the Red Sea plunges from 1,000 meters to deeps of more than 2,000 meters and lies along a tectonic fault zone that forms part of the great interconnected rift system extending from the East African Rift Valley in the south, along the bottom of the Red Sea and up into the Jordan Valley in the north. Shoreward from the central channel, the bed of the Red Sea becomes shallower, with rocky islets and coral reefs advancing far out from the coastline. Extensive shallow areas with well-developed coral growth often result in a complex archipelago of reefs and islands, such as the Farasan banks off the southern Arabian coast. Other island groups occur in deeper water on the seaward extensions of the continental shelf where the Red Sea narrows at its southern end; these islands are based on volcanoes related to the rift system. The Red Sea is also still widening by a few centimeters each year as Arabia drifts further away from the African continent.

Tropical seas differ from temperate seas in that the life they support is much more dependent on the effects of winds, currents, and water clarity. Because of the way in which these factors are balanced, the Red Sea has become famous for its remarkably well developed coral reefs and their spectacular inhabitants.

The major winds affecting the Red Sea region are of two types. Trade winds are caused by rising equatorial temperatures, which create depressions into which the tropic air masses flow and thus cause winds that blow permanently toward the equatorial tropics and cool the coastal regions. The prevailing wind in the Red Sea is north-northwest, although this direction is reversed in the winter in the south. Monsoons are recurring winds that change direction with the seasons; in winter they blow from the high-pressure zones over the land out toward the ocean, and in summer they draw breezes into low-pressure zones of overheated air over land masses. The northwestern monsoons account for the winter

A limestone cliff north of Jeddah showing the dark stripe of blue-green algae. (*Kit Constable-Maxwell*)

and spring high tides by pushing water into the Red Sea through the Straits of Bab al Mandab, and the southwestern monsoons create an eastward-moving current that draws water out of the Red Sea. Very high temperatures also increase the rate of evaporation in summer, thus the winter sea level can be between 0.5 and 1 meter higher than the summer level. The narrowness of the Red Sea and its irregular coastline also account for the fact that its currents are more easily influenced by local winds than those in larger bodies of water.

Because the waters of the central Red Sea are calm and do not have a very large daily tide, there is always some period when the reef fish can graze undisturbed on the algae on the reef crest; this grazing may contribute to the absence of calcareous algal ridges like those seen on coral

Two Red Sea Venus combs: *Murex tribulus. (Kit Constable-Maxwell)*

reef crests elsewhere in the world. There is, however, an oscillatory movement of the water whereby the northern end experiences a high tide while the southern end has a low tide, and vice versa. In the Gulfs of Suez and Aqaba this daily water oscillation causes tides of 0.6 to 1.4 meters.

Ocean currents can affect the environment by moving gigantic quantities of water and spreading the eggs of tropical molluscan species from a relatively restricted area of only about 30° latitude over a zone of 80° latitude. Because the Red Sea is semi-enclosed, one would not expect such currents to affect it, but, in fact, much of its marine life seems to have originated in the Indian Ocean. Many species are not suited to this rather limited environment, and, as a consequence, fewer varieties of animals are found there. There is, however, no lack of animal life in the Red Sea because some of its species occur in great abundance. The possibility that endemic (unique) species will occur in the Red Sea is enhanced because of its semi-enclosed, nearly isolated position, its warmer temperature, and its slightly increased salinity. At present, it is estimated that between 10 and 20 per cent of all molluscan species in the Red Sea are endemic; the figure for some smaller groups, such as cowries, approaches 40 per cent.

The maximum depth at which corals normally live depends on the water's clarity, for those algae symbiotically associated with corals must have light to convert carbon dioxide and water into food substances. Shallow areas containing a large amount of sediment are not conducive to good coral growth because the light cannot penetrate the cloudy water. There is little coral growth either in the Gulf of Suez in the northwest or in the extreme south below the main ports of Massawa in Ethiopia and Hodaidah in Yemen because these areas are comparatively shallow and cloudy. Elsewhere, well-developed reefs flourish. The reefs in the Gulf of Aqaba are, in fact, the most northerly, fully developed reefs in the world, perhaps because the cloudless sky's sun warms the sea even more than could normally be expected at such latitudes. Coral-impeding sediment is also minimal owing to the lack of inflowing streams. Four basic types of reef can be recognized in the Red Sea—fringing reefs, barrier reefs, atolls, and patch reefs.

Fringing reefs are elongated, shallow-water reefs 50 meters to 1 kilometer from and usually parallel to the shore and extending in an almost unbroken line for several kilometers, most commonly in the northern and central areas of the Red Sea. These reefs are often young, and their most intense growth is on the seaward side. Often present on the coastal side of the reefs are still-water lagoons where all but the most hardy, slow-growing species of coral die off as their skeletons are broken down by animals and waves. Well-established fringing reefs broken by the eroded cuts of wadis (which can be several kilometers in width and are known as *sharm* in Arabic) are found on both sides of the Red Sea and harbor a rich concentration of intricate branching corals and several types of dome coral. These inlets are punctuated by small crevices, fissures, and caves that offer shelter to fishes and invertebrates. As the bottoms of some of these are as much as 50 meters below the present sea level, they were perhaps formed when the sea was lower.

An aerial view of reefs in the Red Sea. (*Gunnar Bemert*)

Barrier reefs, a more mature type of reef found from 2 to 10 kilometers offshore, are elongated like the fringing reefs and also are more or less parallel to the shore. Comprising many complex forms, they are sometimes continuous but can vary enormously; fringing reefs, patch reefs, and islands sometimes occur between them and the shore. Reef complexes that can be equated with a form of barrier reef exist opposite the coast just north of Jeddah and opposite the bay of Al Wajh. The Sudan also has a fairly continuous series of such barrier reef complexes.

Atolls arise from deep water, are roughly circular, and have steep outer sides and a shallow central lagoon. Passes or cuts in the ring allow great volumes of tidal waters to flow through. There are only a few deep-water reefs of this type in the Red Sea. One example is the Sanganab Reef northeast of Port Sudan.

Patch reefs are small flat-topped hills with sloping sides. This type of reef tends to occur in depths as shallow as 1.5 meters (typically with an open sand and eelgrass bottom).

It should be noted that, as with a great many scientific terms, the exact way in which any reef name is applied may vary from scientist to scientist. In fact, a single reef might go through several of the different forms described above during its development.

All reefs are divided into zones, each zone having different species of flora and fauna according to its environmental properties. For example, brightly colored gorgonian fans and soft corals are found at depth because they do not require a great deal of light and can colonize near-vertical surfaces. The ways in which environmental conditions combine with the development of plant and animal communities vary; thus, distinct zones appear at different depths and positions across the reef. These zones of the sea and how they function as habitats will be discussed in a following chapter.

When winds, currents, and water clarity are in their optimum states, tropical seas will be extremely conducive to the maximum growth of animal life.

The Arabian Gulf

Unlike the Red Sea, which is a fairly deep trough to the west of the Arabian Peninsula, the Arabian Gulf is a shallow, east-dipping platform that is an extension of the Peninsula covered by water and forming a huge inland sea. It lies northwest–southeast, its only opening being at the narrow Strait of Hormuz, which restricts the inflow of Indian Ocean waters. Apart from a trough lying parallel to and in front of the Zagros Mountains on its eastern coast, the Gulf is nowhere deeper than 100 meters, its average depth being only 35 meters. Because of this extreme shallowness, its waters undergo rapid temperature changes, both daily and seasonally. The surface temperatures of coastal water can vary from 10°C to 36°C; offshore temperatures range from 15°C to 34°C. Strong winds frequently and thoroughly mix the water, which results in only small vertical variations in water temperatures.

The land masses surrounding the Gulf are all arid. Surface evaporation in the Gulf therefore exceeds all input, the result being highly saline waters ranging from 37 parts per thousand at the entrance to 41 parts per thousand at the northwestern end and occasionally reaching 53 to 66 parts per thousand in the partially enclosed inlets and bays of the eastern end; one example, the Gulf of Salwah, lies between Saudi Arabia and the Qatar Peninsula and is nearly cut off from the Arabian Gulf by Bahrain. Owing to the narrowness of the Strait of Hormuz, the high salinity is not greatly affected by the exchange of water with neighboring seas. The Gulf waters move in a pattern in which the salty (and therefore heavier) waters flow out through the bottom of the Strait, while a compensating quantity of lighter, less salty Indian Ocean water flows in on the surface; in total volume, however, the exchange is only modest.

High salinity is one of the most important environmental factors controlling and limiting the occurrence, distribution, and diversity of Gulf marine life.

The Gulf coast of Saudi Arabia is about 450 kilometers long and is divided into several zones. The northernmost zone curves roughly northwest to southeast in a gentle arc from the Kuwaiti border through Ras Tanura, across Bahrain's islands to the northern tip of the Qatar peninsula. Regional daily or twice-daily tides have a maximum range of around 2 meters, and the coastline is exposed to waves generated by the Gulf's prevailing northerly winds.

Coral reefs are common in the shallower parts of this zone, but they differ widely in size and development. On the open coast, reefs grow to the low-tide mark but the diversity of coral species is smaller than it is in reefs in the open sea. In offshore waters, the lower depth limit for continuous coral cover is usually 15 meters, but, in these coastal areas of the Gulf, where waters are more turbid, coral may only grow to depths of 10 meters or less. The predominant type of reef in this part of the Gulf is the relatively small patch or platform reef. When sand bars form on the leeward side of the larger platform reefs, low, flat coral islands are formed which increase the types of habitat and, therefore, the number of species found in this environment. Coral growth tends to proceed in a ringlike fashion, even around single coral heads; in fact, this type of growth is a prominent feature of the reef flats surrounding the coral islands of the Gulf, where there is no real distinction between platform reefs and fringing reefs.

The southernmost section of coast lies between the city of Dammam

A shell collector itself, the Gulf's carrier shell, *Xenophora caperata* has attached many small bivalves and a few *Ancilla* to its upper surface and outer edge which may be an effort to keep it from sinking into the soft substrate or for reinforcement.
(*Kit Constable-Maxwell*)

A sand dune meeting the Arabian Gulf.
(*Kit Constable-Maxwell*)

and the base of the Qatar peninsula, and curves in a southerly direction, therefore being more nearly parallel to the prevailing winds. Much of this part of the coastline lies along the Gulf of Salwah and is protected from wave action not only by its position but by a stretch of extremely shallow water between Saudi Arabia and Bahrain that forms a barrier to tidal water movement. Temperature variation in these shallow waters is greater, and the salinity is high, ranging from 55 parts per thousand around the Gulf of Salwah to 70 parts per thousand in the extreme south. Because of the interacting factors of high salinity, temperature fluctuation, and a large amount of sediment, there are fewer coral reefs in this bay; however, a few large reef structures several kilometers long do exist, in spite of these adverse conditions.

Between the northernmost and southernmost coastal stretches (between Dammam and Ras Tanura) lies an area called Tarut Bay, which in many ways is unique. This area contains extensive tidal flats and grassbeds and is the major shrimp nursery of the Gulf. Although Tarut Bay shares many features with similar bays along the coast, its especially high productivity has made it the object of special study by ARAMCO marine biologists. This large area of gently sloping, sandy bottom is ideal for shrimps and the development of seagrass beds, but the high sediment context and salinity and the wide temperature variation make it unsuitable for the development of coral reefs.

2 Seashells

What they are

Shells are the homes made and inhabited by backboneless (invertebrate) animals called molluscs, a word which means soft-bodied. Shell (or, more correctly, molluscan) fauna includes not only sea creatures but also the species that live in fresh water (approximately half of all molluscs) and the vast numbers that live on land. Although sand dollars and sea urchins are thought by novices to be shells because they have external shells and no internal backbones, they differ in other biological characteristics and are actually related to starfish (echinoderms). There are other kinds of shells in the world—eggshells, coconut shells, tortoiseshells, and so on—but this volume is concerned only with seashells, those marine molluscs that inhabit the seas and shores, and especially those of Saudi Arabia.

Molluscs are a vital, important part of the ecology and economy of the sea. Some serve as a main food source for economically important food fish, but many others are a direct source of protein for man. Some molluscs are destructive to man and his handiwork. The *Teredo* shipworm clam, for example, has wielded a devastating power resulting in great loss of ships and revenues in past centuries. Man has collected shells, not only for food but also for adornment, for useful materials and implements, or merely for their beauty.

Lovers of beauty respond to the natural shells of molluscan animals, the cameos made from them, and the pearls that they "manufacture" for man. The Roman elite collected shells as playthings, and, by the Renaissance, shells were treasured collectors' items in Europe. By virtue of its connections with the East Indies, the Netherlands became the center of the shell trade. The first illustrated shell books were published in the late 17th Century, and, a century later, the first specimens from the central Pacific and Australasia arrived in Europe. New species were found, and many lavish books appeared in the 19th Century. Collectors increased, but neither collectors nor authors were scientifically inclined, and the collections were the result of buying and selling through dealers. The end of the 19th Century, however, saw an awakening of scientific interest in shells although after World War I, the center of activity moved to the United States. International exchange became even more widespread after World War II soldiers returned home from overseas, and shell collecting became a popular hobby. Snorkeling and scuba diving increased the possibilities for shell collectors, and the concomitant development of underwater cameras kindled a desire to know more about the animal inside the shell. Consequently, its biology, habits, and

Bursa sp., clearly showing the animal's foot. The operculum on the upper surface is out of the way when moving. (*I. Sharabati*)

habitats are now under serious study. With each link in the biological chain that man understands, the general chain grows stronger, and new advances in the field of marine conservation can be made.

GENERAL BIOLOGY OF MOLLUSCS

The branch of zoology that deals only with the forms and descriptions of the hard parts of shells is called conchology (from the Latin word *concha*, or shell), and those who pursue this study are known as conchologists. The branch that deals with molluscs, the soft animals within the shells, is called malacology from the Latin *mollis* and Greek *malakos*, or soft). Scientists who study molluscs as living animals, including the numerous types that do not have shells, are called malacologists.

The phylum of invertebrates called Molluscs is the second largest in the animal kingdom, being surpassed only by Arthropoda (insects). There are approximately 47,000 species of mollusc, ranging in size from a few millimeters to more than 20 meters in length. They are divided into seven classes, although only five are commonly seen. Although their body forms vary from primitive to highly developed, they do have many common features. They are, in fact, a prime example of diversity in nature, for the animals within this single group can and have successfully adapted so that they not only survive but also flourish in most conditions on Earth—from sea slugs, which live 6,000 meters below the sea's surface to terrestrial snails, which live 5,000 meters above sea level at the snowline of the Himalayas.

Molluscs have two basic parts. The body mass (visceral hump) always remains inside and protected by the shell, if one is present. The sensory and feeding apparatus (in the head area) and the organ for locomotion (foot) extend from the shell. Even with only a few elements, molluscan anatomy is very flexible and usually reflects the mode of living to which a particular species must adapt and its method of locomotion.

Molluscs are characterized by two parts of their anatomy that are not found in any other invertebrate. One of these unique organs, the mantle, is a fold of membrane from the body wall that falls in a thin, fleshy cape on either side of the soft body of the animal. Usually, the mantle secretes a protective calcareous (limey) shell into which the body can retract, if it is shaped like a single coil or a pair of valves. The shell may occasionally be composed of eight plates, it may be internal or it may be absent altogether. The shell is usually attached to the animal by a strong muscle, and if the animal is removed, the shell will cease to grow or undergo natural repairs, and the horny protective covering on the outside (the periostracum) will become dry and brittle.

The visceral hump is the center of the molluscan metabolism and contains most of the digestive, circulatory, reproductive, and excretory organs. The mantle is considered by some to be technically a part of the visceral hump, but because its variations often help to define different classes, it is useful to consider it as a separate entity. Between the mantle and the visceral mass is the mantle cavity, which normally houses the external openings of the digestive, excretory, and reproductive organs. In the mantle cavity of most molluscs, featherlike structures called gills

The thrush cowrie (*Cypraea turdus*), a wanderer by day, is seemingly immune to predators.
Picture right, shows this cowrie effectively camoflaged with the mantle fully extended.

Picture below right, the mantle has been partially retracted exposing the shell's surface. (*I. Sharabati*)

are used for oxygenating the blood. Clean, well-oxygenated water is circulated through the mantle cavity by the beating action of cilia, small hairlike structures on the gills, which keeps the water moving across their surfaces. All molluscs except one class (Scaphopoda) have gills, the bivalves using them not only for breathing but also for filtering food from the water. Undigested food and waste products are also washed out by these currents of water passing through the mantle cavity, and reproductive materials are conveyed into the water. Near the front of the

The fragile partridge tun (*Tonna perdix*) usually lives in fairly deep water and is seldom seen except as broken pieces of shell on a beach—Red Sea specimen. (*Angie Pridgen*)

mantle cavity are often sensory organs that can analyze the water and tell the mollusc whether food or foe lies ahead.

The mollusc's head and foot are able to withdraw into the mantle cavity when it is threatened. Below the mantle and extensible from the shell is the enlarged, flat, muscular, solelike organ called the foot. The foot is often powerful and usually aids in clinging or crawling by means of ciliary waves or muscular contractions. However, it is the mantle cavity that has been modified to aid some molluscs' jet propulsive form of locomotion. The foot in clams is greatly reduced or absent, and, in some gastropods, it has been modified into a digging apparatus.

The head is also extensible and includes the eyes, the tentacles, and a short snout bearing the mouth opening and the radula, the other organ that is unique to molluscs. Again, the squids and octopuses are different, their heads being modified into a circle of flexible arms with powerful suckers. The bivalves have lost their heads altogether, for they filter their food from the water with their gills and have no radula at all. The radula, when it is present, is a kind of toothed tongue bearing many microscopic hooklike teeth and is used like a flexible rasp to file off pieces of food, much like a cat's tongue. Just visible to the naked eye and appearing to be the same size as a cotton thread, the radula enables chitons and limpets to grate off encrusting algaes, and winkles to browse on seaweeds. Most bizarre of all, cones have modified their radula into a poison-tipped dart with which they can kill other molluscs and even spear fast-moving fish. Because the radular structure is usually different in various molluscs, it often determines the identification of a species. The positions, sizes, and relationships between the various body organs help to differentiate between the classes and species of mollusc. This has always been the case and thus also aids understanding of molluscan development from fossil samples.

FOSSILS

No fossil molluscs have yet been found that predate the late Precambrian period over 600,000,000 years ago, perhaps only because molluscs were at that time shell-less wormlike creatures that decomposed readily after dying and left no trace of their existence.

The oldest known molluscan fossils are members of the classes Monoplacophora, Bivalvia, and Gastropoda appearing in Lower Cambrian rocks. It can never be proved conclusively that the time sequence of fossils follows their actual appearance in the world, the next evidence of molluscs is nautiloid cephalopod fossils found in Upper Cambrian rocks. With the appearance of the scaphopods in Ordovician times, 425,000,000 to 500,000,000 years ago, six of the present-day classes of mollusc were in existence. Because it is the shelled animals that most commonly leave fossils, it is perhaps understandable that there are none from the seventh class, the aplacophores.

It was in the Ordovician era some 400,000,000 years ago that the cephalopods had their heyday. There were then at least 10,000 species in 600 genera in comparison with today's fewer than 500 species in 150 genera. Some of their fossilized ammonite shells are well known, for they

A close-up of a fossilized mollusc.
(*Heather Ross*)

are currently popular as decorators' objects. Others must have been amazing, for they were more than 4 meters in diameter (up to 11 meters long if uncoiled!).

CLASSIFYING SHELLS

Before the classes of mollusc are described, a note on the system of classification will be helpful.

Taxonomy is the method by which the thousands of different species are arranged into various groups, each of which includes those animals having broadly similar characteristics. Each species has two basic names, in addition to a position in the greater framework of the animal kingdom, much as people do; these two names are the genus and the species.

The species, the smallest grouping, comprises all those animals of one kind that resemble each other so closely that they are practically identical. These individuals, under similar external conditions and in comparative developmental stages, show similar anatomical and physiological characteristics and breed with one another by natural means over several generations. Individuals of the same species produce fertile offspring similar to themselves, whereas mating that does not normally occur between different species usually results in sterile offspring.

The genus, which begins with a capital letter, comes first; the more specific or individual name follows and begins with a lower-case letter. Both of these names are in Latin and are conventionally underlined when they are written or italicized when they are printed. Related genera of mollusc are grouped into families that can contain visibly dissimilar species belonging to various genera but grouped together because of anatomical or behavioral similarities. Superfamilies are a higher grouping usually used only in extensive museum collections. Families and superfamilies are then grouped into orders, and orders are grouped into classes. There are seven classes of mollusc in the phylum Mollusca.

The binomial (two-name) system of classifying shells is universally accepted and because it is in Latin serves as a common denominator in consulting literature and placing shells in their proper places in a collection. Each molluscan species has its own niche within a genus, family, order, and class. Aristotle and his contemporaries called octopus, squid, and sea slugs Mollusca or Malakia. All marine snails, slugs, and bivalves were called Testacea or Ostracoderma. It was not until the 18th Century that comparative anatomical study found the internal anatomy of both groups to be similar; henceforth, only a single phylum, Mollusca, was necessary.

The two-part name often has a third added to it, the name of the scientist or author who first described and named that particular species. The first-described specimen is called the holotype and is usually placed in a museum collection for further reference. Other (if any) specimens found at the same time and place as the holotype, and that were in front of the author when he was preparing the original description of the species, are called the paratypes and are often deposited in collections belonging to different museums to ensure that the "types" are readily available to as many scientists as possible.

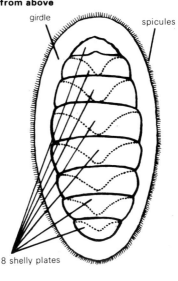

Monoplacophora

shell

gills

foot

mouth   head

**Polyplacophora (chiton)
from above**

girdle   spicules

8 shelly plates

SEVEN CLASSES OF MOLLUSC

MONOPLACOPHORA

Monoplacophora, the most primitive species of shell, was known only from fossils until 1952, when the first live limpetlike specimen was brought up from 3,500 meters by a Danish expedition off the coast of Costa Rica. The small (2.5 to 4 centimeter) caplike shell was named *Neopilina galatheae* after the vessel *Galathea* that brought it up. About 10 living species have now been identified, as new samples have been dredged up from trenches up to 6,400 meters deep in several different oceans. *Neopilina* is still extremely scarce, although it has not been determined if the scarcity is due to rarity or to the difficulty in collecting it. This mollusc was known previously only from a diverse number of fossil species from the Lower Cambrian–Middle Devonian strata of approximately 375,000,000 years ago and was thought to have been extinct since that time. Although it looks exactly like a limpet with a broad foot dominating the undersurface of its body, *Neopilina* was discovered to be quite different. It has the uniquely molluscan characteristic of having some of its internal organs serially repeated. This apparent segmentation perhaps provides a link between the molluscs and the segmented worms and insect invertebrates.

APLACOPHORA

Aplacophora, an exclusively marine class of wormlike mollusc, numbers around 250 species. It has a worldwide distribution ranging from shallow waters to depths of 4,000 meters, and is bottom dwelling at any depth, usually burrowing into the soft sediments. One of the aplacophora reaches a length of 30 centimeters, but most species are very small and feed on organic debris and microscopic organisms, although some are found among algae, hydroids, and corals. Aplacophora has no shell, but the mantle rolls in to enclose the body, and its surface is covered with a cuticle in which calcareous spicules are embedded like microscopic scales, often giving it a silvery appearance. It generally has several features characteristic of molluscs, including a simple radula, an elementary mantle cavity, and a reduced but typically molluscan foot. The solenogasters used to be grouped with the chitons into a single class called Amphineura and may have shared a common ancestry, but they have diverged greatly and are no longer grouped together.

POLYPLACOPHORA

The approximately 600 species of the primitive Polyplacophora are usually called chitons and are very common to all seas. Usually small (although one North American species is about 35 centimeters long) their most notable feature is an articulated shell of eight plates (valves), which over-lap like shingles and enable them to roll up into a ball for protection. These calcareous plates, from which their nickname of "coat-of-mail shells" derives, cover the entire back and at the edge are embedded in the leathery, flexible, ringlike part of the mantle called a "girdle." Chitons lack tentacles and eyes but have other microsensory organs in the shell and girdle surfaces. Chitons are often found together with limpets on the rocky shores of the intertidal areas which they inhabit. Being sensitive to light, they venture out of their cracks and crevices at night to browse on algae, crawling along on their broad foot at a rate of 1 to 15 centimeters per minute by means of transverse backward waves within their muscular, suckerlike foot. Due to the foot's ability to create a vacuum effect and to secrete a sticky mucous lubrication, they are extremely difficult to pry off their rocky habitats.

GASTROPODA

Gastropoda, the largest and most diverse class of living mollusc, and perhaps the best known, numbers approximately 37,500 living species and represents some 80 per cent of living molluscs. More than half of these snails and slugs are marine varieties, and it is the only class to have spread both into freshwater and on to land. Although the much-sought-after gastropod shells vary enormously, their soft parts are similar in structure, and consequently they are classified together. The variations and special adaptations of their bodies are especially evident in their locomotory and feeding mechanisms and reflect a wide range of habitats.

The name gastropod means an animal that "crawls on its stomach." This impression may be given by the large, flat, muscular foot, which is used to creep about by creating a series of muscular waves and secreting a mucus that temporarily cements together the particles of sand and gives them a carpet on which to slide. Although it is often modified in burrowing or swimming forms, the foot of most gastropods has an operculum, a horny or calcareous plate similar in shape to the shell's aperture and used to close it, to dig, to aid in locomotion, or even to be swung and used as a weapon. It can also be important in identifying and classifying a shell.

The simplest gastropods have paired gills. The primitive groups of limpets merely draw water in under the shell and pump it over the gills and back out under the edge of the shell. Keyhole limpets and abalones have separate holes in the shell through which the used water is expelled. Members of a more advanced group inhale water through a siphon and can therefore still have oxygenated water while they feed on decomposing matter. In the most developed forms, there is a tendency for one or both gills to be absent; in such cases, gases are exchanged either through the body surface or through specially developed respiratory structures.

Gastropods have well-developed heads with tentacles and often highly-developed eyes. They usually have a mouth with a radula, and their mode of feeding is often reflected in the number and formation of the radular teeth. For example, herbivorous molluscs such as the most primitive group of limpets, tops, nerites, and abalones rasp at vegetable matter with a radula of hard mineralized teeth arranged in rows of more than 100. Omnivorous shells such as cowries have seven teeth in each row that allow them to cut or scrape food particles off the substrate. Carnivorous molluscs, including whelks and volutes, have only three teeth in a row, which is sufficient for the softer tissues of their diet. One carnivore has a radula equipped with a replaceable harpoonlike tooth with which

Gastropoda

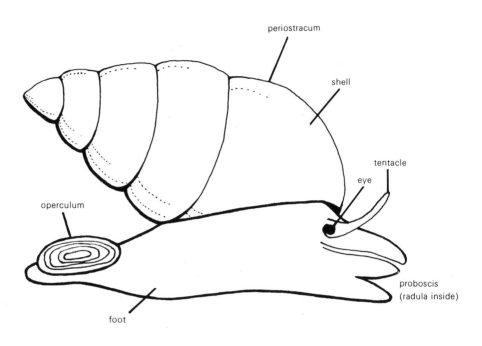

he injects a nerve poison that paralyzes his prey, before ingesting it whole. Parasitic gastropods that suck the juices of molluscs or other invertebrates have no radula at all. Some carnivorous species which prey on thick-shelled molluscs, have gizzards with strong shelly plates and spines that crush and grind up ingested shells.

There are three subclasses of gastropod. The most highly developed group is the lung-bearing air-breathing Pulmonata. Except for a few marine species (such as *Siphonaria*) this group is land-dwelling and so will not be further discussed in this book.

The Prosobranchia are asymmetric and are complicated by an extraordinary twisting torsion of 180° that happens during the life of the veliger larva. The main nerve cord, originally a simple loop, becomes a "figure-of-eight," and the one or two gills in the mantle cavity move to a position in front of the heart. All living gastropods at some developmental stage (usually the larval) undergo this torsion, but the prosobranchs retain this configuration.

A few shell-less sea slugs, bubble shells, and their relatives undergo a second partial reversal of torsion that results in a single gill behind the heart in the mantle cavity; members of this group become the "rear gills," Opisthobranchia. There is some debate as to the real purpose of this torsion, but most authorities agree that it has nothing to do with the spiral coiling of the shell. One plausible theory is that before torsion, the molluscan head is the last part of the animal to be withdrawn into the shell and therefore the most vulnerable, whereas, after torsion, the head is withdrawn first, and the less vital foot and its hard operculum withdraw last, closing off the aperture like a door. A secondary theory is that the post-torsion position of the mantle cavity containing exits from the gut and excretory organs, places the gills in a better position to receive an unimpaired oxygen supply. Both the prosobranchs and the opisthobranchs are mostly marine species and live everywhere, but the greater number are found on rocky, sandy, and muddy bottoms in the littoral (seashore) areas. At increased depths, the number of species in this sub-class decreases.

Many marine prosobranchs have well-developed shells produced by the mantle as additions to the shell's edge. The oldest part of the shell is the apex or tip, which may be lost at a later stage of development. Opposite the apical end is the base, which may extend into a siphonal canal. The aperture (opening) may be circular, oval, angular, or have a narrow or broad slit, and both its inner and outer edges may have many configurations such as teeth, callouses, folds, tubercles, or spines. Shells are normally coiled dextrally (clockwise); sinistrally (counter-clockwise) coiled shells, rare in most species, are nevertheless common in a very few. The shape and ornamentation of a shell often correlate with its owner's habits. The opisthobranch, mostly sea slugs, appear bilaterally symmetrical, at least externally, and the shell is often reduced and frequently covered by parts of the mantle or foot; in more advanced forms, the shell may be absent altogether.

Prosobranchs may be divided further into three orders. The most primitive group, archaeogastropods means "old gastropod" and contains simple shells, usually cone shaped without an operculum or spirally coiled with an operculum. Members of this order often have holes or notches and very simple mantle cavities that take in water from around their edges to the feathery gills; as a result, they are especially prone to clogging by salt and sediment. For this reason, they avoid sandy areas and are found on rocky shores or on the forereef and its face, mostly feeding on the algae prevalent in these same areas. The interiors of their shells are usually lined with mother-of-pearl. The order includes the familiar limpets, abalones, tops, and turbans.

The "middle gastropods" (Mesogastropoda) are found in a variety of habitats because of their many specialized adaptations. They have a more advanced organization of the mantle cavity than the archaeogastropods as well as other features that allow the sand dwellers among them to cope more effectively with sediment (for example, the siphon is often situated in a special groove on the anterior edge of the shell's aperture). Their shell is usually spirally coiled with a horny operculum and lacks a mother-of-pearl layer. The many algae feeders have short, mobile snouts and a radula that characteristically has seven teeth in every transverse row. Mesogastropods include the periwinkles, ceriths, wentletraps, conchs and strombs, moon snails, cowries, helmets and bonnets, tuns, and tritons.

Many species of the biologically advanced group of molluscs, Neogastropoda ("new gastropods") are also especially adapted to life on or in sandy-bottomed habitats. This group includes a variety of families,

Clockwise: *Conus virgo, C. omaria*, two *C. textile*, and two color variations of *C. striatus*—Red Sea specimens. (*Kit Constable-Maxwell*)

most of which are carnivorous predators feeding on other gastropods, bivalves, worms, and fish.

There are two suborders of neogastropod, differentiated (among other things) by their radula. Members of the first group (Stenoglossa) have a proboscis (snout) with a narrow radula containing not more than three teeth in each row. A siphon extends from an opening of the mantle cavity above the head of the animal and draws water down into the gills from above the level of the sand and sediment. It also moves in various directions, testing the water as it enters the mantle cavity by means of a sense organ that has become an important chemosensory apparatus for smelling the presence of prey. This group includes the sand-dwelling olives, harps, volutes, margins, miters, and murexes.

Members of the second suborder of neogastropod are called Toxoglossa. Some species (such as Terebridae) have no teeth; some Turridae have 3 or 5 teeth in a row, and cones have a radula with only 2 rows of grooved harpoonlike teeth used to inject poison into their prey. There are three major well-known families in this group, the augers, the cones,

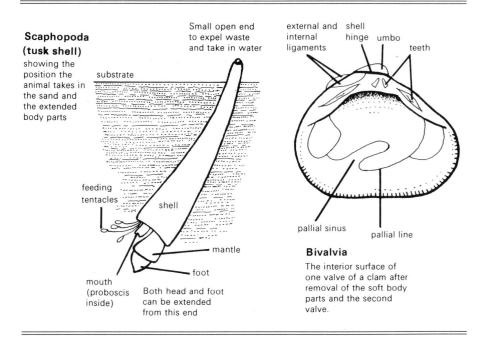

Scaphopoda (tusk shell) showing the position the animal takes in the sand and the extended body parts

substrate

Small open end to expel waste and take in water

feeding tentacles

shell

mantle

foot

mouth (proboscis inside)

Both head and foot can be extended from this end

external and internal ligaments

shell hinge

umbo

teeth

pallial sinus

pallial line

Bivalvia The interior surface of one valve of a clam after removal of the soft body parts and the second valve.

and the turrids. These carnivorous sand dwellers are active at the turn of the tide and leave an easily seen trail on the bottom.

The gastropods have exploited many ecological niches and therefore are of many diverse shapes and sizes. Many groups, especially intertidal species, are capable of complicated and variable responses to their environment.

SCAPHOPODA

There are about 350 species of Scaphopoda, the simplest marine shells, which resemble elephant tusks. Although uncommon they are the easiest class of shell to identify. Most are from fairly deep water, but their shells are strong, and so they are frequently washed up into shallow water or onto the shore. Usually white and ribbed and 2 to 12 centimeters long, the cylindrical, slightly curved, one-piece tapering tube is open at both ends. Both the head and the foot project from the larger end and remain below the mud or sand. The shell is slanted upward, with the tip of the narrower end protruding from the sand, so that water can be pumped into the mantle cavity through the narrow opening for respiration. The foot is the most vital organ, as it aids in feeding and is also a means of locomotion, anchoring, and burrowing. Scaphopods move by extending the foot, expanding it with blood to act as an anchor, and pulling the shell along by the muscular contraction of the foot.

BIVALVIA

Bivalves, also known as pelecypods ("hatchet footed"), are the second largest class of mollusc and number about 7,500 species. Although bivalves are less numerous than the class Gastropoda, they are of greater economic value—clams, oysters, scallops, and mussels are eaten, and in addition pearls are either found or "farmed" in oysters. All bivalves are aquatic, and many are marine species, being found anywhere from intertidal areas to great depths. The majority are bottom living and are associated with sand and mud, although several have adapted to hard bottoms.

The bivalve body is bilaterally flattened, and nearly all are enclosed within two calcareous valves that can be either identical or dissimilar. The hinge between these two pieces may have teeth with corresponding sockets; the two valves are connected and kept slightly open by the resilient action of a flexible ligament but can be firmly closed by one or two strong adductor muscles. Each valve has a protuberance on the dorsal surface called a "beak" or "umbo," which is the oldest part of the shell. Bivalves do not have a head, sense organs, or a radula, although some species have eyes on the mantle margins.

The mantle hangs down on either side of the body like two curtains, and the shell is secreted by the mantle's outer surface along its edge. The mantle cavity is very enlarged, as are the gills, which, in addition to their respiratory function, act as food filters, for bivalves feed on particles of plankton and other microscopic organisms suspended in the seawater. Enormous quantities of water are pumped in and out of the mantle cavity for this food-filtration process through two tubular siphons formed by a modification of the posterior end of the mantle. The common mussel (*Mytilus edulis*), for example, filters about 1.5 liters per hour, and one oyster (*Crassostrea virginica*) can filter up to 37 liters per hour. Other bivalves suck in microscopic food particles, such as worms and small invertebrates, from the seabed via their inhalent siphon. The mantle margins of deep burrowers extend to form enormous muscular siphons

Related to the giant clam (*Tridacna*), this tiny *T. squamosa* is a miniature (4 cm.) frilled version with a colorful mantle—Red Sea specimen. (*I. Sharabati*)

Cephalopoda

Sepia (cuttlefish)

Side view showing
undulating fin and
chambered cuttlebone

cuttlefish bone

eye

fin

collar

tentacles

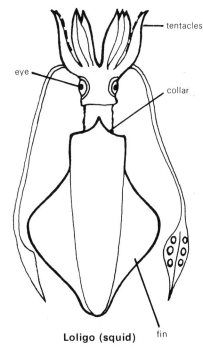

tentacles

eye

collar

Loligo (squid)   fin

tentacles

eye

funnel

Octopus

that can equal many times the length of the animal's shell. Not all particles thus taken in are passed along to the gut to be digested; some are rejected by a sorting process and expelled with the water being pumped out. The giant clams (*Tridacna maxima*) cultivate small algae to be used as food within their own shells.

The foot in burrowers such as clams is well developed and has been altered into an efficient digging apparatus. In some oysters, the foot is much reduced because they cement themselves firmly to one spot for most of their lives. Other groups, such as mussels, use a gland in their foot to secrete byssus threads for anchoring. A very few bivalves, such as scallops, live unattached on the bottom and can "swim" away from danger with a kind of jet propulsion created by opening and closing their valves.

Bivalves generally grow by adding to the edges of the valves opposite the hinge. There is some question about their longevity, but oysters probably live between 10 and 15 years, with pearl oysters possibly living as long as 60 years.

CEPHALOPODA

The most highly developed and active class of mollusc is undoubtedly the cephalopods, which are exclusively marine and include around 600 species. Their size is extremely variable, ranging from tiny species just 15 millimeters long to giant squid 18 meters long, the largest known species of any invertebrate animal. Cephalopods, including the famous chamber-shelled nautilus, the internal-shelled squid and cuttlefish, and the shell-less octopus, have well-developed sensory organs, especially the eyes. Their senses are linked to an intelligent brain with a capacity to learn. All are carnivorous and have several modifications that help them to be fast and efficient hunters.

Cephalopods have no obvious foot, but they have developed two

Squid hover in midwater, near or above reefs . . . and are often grouped into "shoals."
(*Angie Pridgen, John O'Dell*)

other altered structures; arms and tentacles equipped with suckers surround the mouth, and a funnel or siphon has been formed from the foot and mantle cavity. The head end of the mantle has a free border called the collar. Water enters the mantle cavity around the edge of this collar and is rapidly ejected through the funnel as the mantle contracts and seals the collar against the body. This process produces the famous "jet propulsion" of the cephalopods. Powerful jaws, a parrot-like beak for tearing at flesh, and a radula complete the basic characteristics required for speedy predation. Because they have lost their protective shells, their sharp senses and ability to move fast afford some measure of protection against their enemies, which include fish, seals, sea lions, and whales. Another defensive mechanism, a sac opening into the mantle cavity, releases ink that has a repelling smell as well as a visually confusing action. The skin of a cephalopod is unique, for it can change its color, pattern, and even its texture, not only to match its surroundings for camouflage, as is commonly believed, but also to match its emotional mood. An octopus will, for example, "blush" when it is fed its favorite food. Although all cephalopods can swim, some prefer other modes of locomotion, and they are found at nearly all depths.

Body shapes, all bilaterally symmetrical, are the means by which the different species can be identified. Free-swimming squid, which usually live in groups, are essentially pointed torpedo shapes with triangular lateral fins used for stabilization extending from both sides. The cuttlefish have flattened oval bodies with ribbonlike fins running their length. The body is strengthened internally by a calcareous shell, the cuttlefish bone, that contains a series of very narrow chambers filled with gas or fluid and that can be pumped full or emptied to serve as hydrostatic equipment for swimming or floating. Cuttlefish live in coastal waters among vegetation, lying on sandy bottoms partly buried in the sand and swimming only at night in search of their preferred diet of shrimps and crabs.

The octopus is a crawling form of solitary cephalopod, living most of its life in the rocky substrata of caves and crevices by day and coming out to feed at night. Its globular body is slightly indented where it joins the head, and its long tentacles are located around its parrotlike beak. One octopus (*Argonauta*) secretes a thin shell-like receptacle for its eggs called a paper nautilus, but, although this structure is coiled and rigid, it is not a shell. The *Nautilus*, which has the famous chambered shell, crawls above the mud of the sea bottom looking for edible crabs and shellfish and uses the buoyancy of its gas-filled chambers to rise from the depths.

How they live

The basics necessary to all molluscs include finding food, seeking protection, and reproducing their own kind.

REPRODUCTION AND GROWTH

Molluscs exhibit various methods of reproduction; this distinguishes them from other invertebrates, which reproduce in only one way. It is believed that the early primitive univalves and bivalves had separate sexes without accessible sex organs and that they discharged their ova and sperm into the seawater for external fertilization. Many present-day molluscs have retained this method of reproduction, although it is highly subject to predation. To offset this danger, these species either lay enormous numbers of eggs or have special means of protecting them. Because the sperm are diluted in the sea, methods of increasing the efficiency of fertilization have also evolved. For example, some limpets and tops do not release their eggs unless they are near other shells of the same species. (Just how they know that other shells are near has not been determined.)

Many advanced gastropods and cephalopods practice copulation between the two sexes, the result being internal fertilization. Some species, on the other hand, do not have separate sexes. The sea hares and the nudibranch sea slugs (and most air-breathing land snails) are hermaphrodites, each animal having the capacities of both sexes. Two animals come together, exchange sperm, part, and each produces young. Other species of marine mollusc exhibit sex changes during their lifetime. The common oyster (*Ostrea edulis*) begins as a male, changes into a female to lay eggs, and, after shedding its eggs, reverts to being a male. The slipper limpet (*Crepidula fornicata*) lives in chains of up to 12. The topmost and youngest are males, the middle individuals are in some stage

A rosette of nudibranch eggs.
(*Gunnar Bemert*)

of change between male and female, and the larger numbers at the bottom are the females. If a female (which normally exudes a female hormone) dies, the hormone level in the surrounding water drops, and a male further up in the chain will change into a female within a week.

Despite the great differences in external appearances among adult members of the major classes of mollusc, all develop from only a few different types of larva. Most commonly, molluscan eggs hatch into top-shaped larva (trochophores), which have a ring of cilia around the middle and a tuft on top. They resemble annelid worms and were the chief reason that scientists used to suppose a link between molluscs and annelids before the discovery of *Neopilina*. The trochophore larva may only last a short time and then develop into a veliger larva by growing a pair of long ciliated arms or paddle-shaped lobes for swimming and trapping plankton. The bottom of a veliger larva grows very little, and the top becomes a disproportionally large sac-like body cavity, a configuration which the cephalopods retain. Some species hatch directly into the more advanced veliger larva, possessing a tiny shell (the protoconch), which can often be recognized later at the apex of the mature shell. Later, the larva settles onto the seabed, casts off the velum, and begins life as a tiny replica of an adult of the species. Those species having a long planktonic phase will have a wider distribution, which is especially important to sedentary species such as the attached bivalves as only this free-swimming stage will effect the dispersion of the species. Active molluscs have less need for a pelagic phase or for prodigal reproduction. These species usually have fewer, larger eggs which are often laid in cases that can vary enormously in shape. The eggs, and even sometimes the young, are protected by the female. Some of the eggs develop into embryos, hatch, and emerge as crawling snails.

LOCOMOTION AND FEEDING

Food is necessary for life, and the means of locomotion often affects the success with which food is acquired. Locomotion often dictates possible habitats, which can also determine food availability. The role of mobility will be discussed here; habitat will be dealt with in a following section.

Molluscs can be divided into groups according to types of movement— some are sedentary, others are free swimming, crawling, or burrowing.

The sedentary group includes most of the bivalves that are attached or anchored in one place throughout their adult lives, although they have been, in many cases, mobile in their veliger stage. Molluscs having a veliger stage often reproduce in the spring, when there is more plank-

Lambis truncata sebae. The development of the long, narrow operculum into a horny claw allows the stromb to move or "polevault" over himself by extending the foot, digging in the claw, and contracting the foot. Because of its shape, the operculum can also block the slitlike entrance to the shell.
(*Kit Constable-Maxwell*)

One of the poisonous tented cones (*Conus textile*) showing the siphon (with black and red stripes), proboscis (pink), eyed tentacle (white with black dot), and a portion of the foot. (*D. Sharabati*)

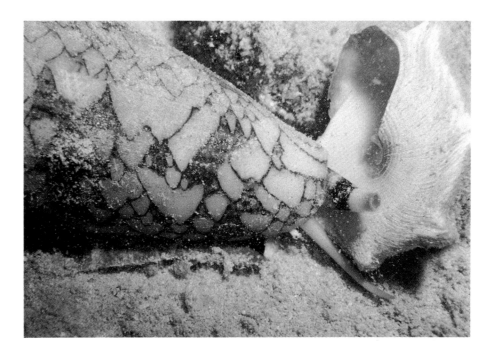

tonic food suspended in the sea, for their food requirements are very high in this phase of development as large amounts of energy are used for swimming and growing. Larvae that develop further settle out of the plankton, but few survive to adulthood because of predation, although their demise probably also constitutes an important ocean energy resource.

By the time they reach adulthood, bivalves are, in most cases, firmly attached to the substratum and feed from their surroundings in one of two ways. The first group, the deposit feeders, use their long inhalant siphons like a vacuum cleaner and suck up the debris resulting from the decomposition of animal, mineral, and vegetable matter in the sea deposited on the sand and mud around them. There is no lack of this detritus, for there is a continuous rain of dead plankton and animal and organic refuse from above. Suspension or filter feeding is the more common method used by bivalves. This combination of breathing and feeding is extremely economical in effort and enables these bivalves to live in crowded conditions and still have an ample supply of food arriving on every tide.

The second type of locomotion used by molluscs is swimming or passively floating. All cephalopods are swimmers, but only a few of the bivalves have any means of waterborne movement—the cockles can jump many centimeters by flexing their strong foot, and scallops move through the water by clapping their two valves together. Among the gastropods, those with little or no shell, like the sea hares and nudibranchs, are found the swimmers and passive floaters. One coil-shelled sea snail (*Janthina*) keeps afloat by secreting from its foot a frothy liquid that hardens on contact with seawater into a raft of bubbles to which it stays attached and floats about.

The largest group of molluscs falls into the wide classification of burrowers and active crawlers. Members of the burrowing group are found in all marine habitats and include all kinds of feeders. In shallow waters, moon snails (*Polinices* and *Natica*) burrow to get to their bivalve prey, while the bivalve cockles (*Cardium*) plough through the sand. In deeper water, razor clams (*Solen*), and tellins (*Tellina*) have an extensible foot that is thrust downward and then expanded at the tip, thereby acting as an anchor against which the shell is pulled down into the sand or mud by the foot's contraction. These bivalves always have two long siphons reaching to the surface to maintain flows of water-borne food and wastes into and out of their mantle cavities. Borers, in contrast, do more than merely move through semi-solid materials such as sand. They actually cut or rasp their way through solid objects. The infamous *Teredo* ship-worm begins as a very tiny bivalve and burrows mechanically as it feeds on the wood of ships' planks or piers, growing larger as it advances through the wood. The date mussel (*Lithophaga*) bores through hard limestone by secreting an acid that helps to dissolve it. The piddock (*Pholas*) bores into any solid substance except the hardest rock. Its shell is thin but extremely hard and armed at the front with rows of spines. By holding on with its foot and alternately contracting and relaxing its two adductor muscles, the piddock rocks its valves back and forth like a mechanical drill. The debris from its burrow is ejected through a special exhalant siphon. It has no eyes or other photosensitive organs of any kind, and some are brilliantly phosphorescent.

Even more active than the burrowers and borers are the crawling molluscs and diverse feeding patterns are found in this group. Many of these gastropods find their food in the substratum and use their radula to rasp or scrape bacteria and fungal or algal film off rock surfaces and to tear away plant material from corals and sponges. These grazers are in the majority, but many marine gastropods are carnivorous and use their modified radulae to attack their prey, boring holes in sea urchins and other shells and sucking out their contents, or enwrapping and prying open bivalves. Perhaps the most famous of these predators is the Triton's trumpet (*Charonia tritonus*), which feeds on the equally infamous Crown-of-Thorns starfish. Cone shells, the most active and efficient predators, locate their prey (often bottom-living fish such as gobies and blennies) by scent. A cone's radula is formed of spearlike teeth, one of which protrudes from the end of its proboscis and after stalking their prey, they harpoon them and paralyze them with a nerve poison.

The most active and most aggressive of the molluscs are the cephalopods, all of which are fast moving hunters. The squid will stalk a school of fish, swim in and grab one with its tentacles and quickly take a bite from its neck, and a school of hungry squid can decimate a thousand mackarel in a few minutes. The octopus drags a clam, snail, or crustacean victim over the ground to its lair using its beaked mouth and tentacles with suckers often also armed with horny hooks.

There are other unusual methods of feeding among the various classes. One enterprising vermetid snail, which lives in a burrow in the coral, fishes for plankton with sticky tendrils of mucus that can reach up to a yard in length. One of the most unusual feeding methods of all is that of the giant clam (*Tridacna*) which lies in tropical reefs with its shell gaping and its fleshy edged mantle exposed to the sun, raising a crop of

Two nudibranchs which may represent two different species of dorid: *Chromodoris quadricolor* (the smaller) and *C. africana* (the larger)—Red Sea specimens. (*Angie Pridgen*)

zooxanthellae. Parasitic snails without shells, living in the intestines of sea cucumbers, suck blood directly from the walls of their hosts' guts, and others, embedded in "cysts" in the arms of starfish and sea urchin spines, use their proboscises to tap the hosts' juices. Some molluscs are not at all particular about their diet and will consume dead fish, putrifying molluscs, and decaying vegetable matter. Others seem gluttonous; a nudibranch swallows other univalves whole, and one herbivorous sea hare consumes more than 2 kilograms of seaweed a day.

PROTECTION

How well a mollusc protects itself is a major factor affecting its survival. Mobility (the ability to flee from an enemy), is one means of protection. Another effective defensive mechanism developed by many molluscs is also the most obvious—a strong shell into which they can withdraw when danger threatens. Molluscan shells were probably developed over a long period of time not only as a protection against predators but also against hostile environments. For example, intertidal species in the tropics, which are usually globular and thus have a decreased surface area, rarely have good contact with the ground; consequently, the heat conducted to them through their foot area is reduced. The light-reflecting pale color or the sculptured contours of many molluscs increase the surface's efficiency in radiating heat and so act as methods of temperature control.

There are, however, molluscs that do not make shells, and they also must have means of protecting themselves. Cephalopods, strong swimmers who chase their food in the open sea would be hindered by shells. They have, of course, their mobility and sharp senses to help them escape predators, but some have additional biological and chemical means of defense. Many cephalopods, for example, can release ink into the water to confuse and repel their enemies or change their body color to blend in with their surroundings. The octopus can even change the texture of his skin.

The shell-less species of nudibranch seem to have a variety of defenses at their command. Some expel acids from their skin, and others ingest nematocysts (stinging cells) with their food; in some mysterious way, these cells pass through their digestive systems without ill effect and are later expelled or discharged in an active condition at a hungry predator. Other nudibranchs have calcareous spicules in their skin that make them too prickly to be palatable to fish. The most obvious frilly parts of the nudibranchs often attract a predator and thereby distract it from the more crucial head. Color, too, may serve to warn enemies that this little animal is not for eating, for many of these clownlike creatures are anything but well camouflaged.

Their uses

MAN AND SHELLS IN THE MIDDLE EAST

Man has used shells in many ways for tens of thousands of years. Fragments of semi-fossilized bivalves, murex, cowries, and cuttlefish bone have been found on Ubaid sites in southern Mesopotamia dating from 4300 to 3500 B.C.

Man has eaten almost every species of mollusc at some time or place and they may also have been used as bait, for being generally slow moving they would therefore be easier to catch than would the fish that they were used to tempt. Fishing hooks in Dilmun (present-day Bahrain) were found cut from thin bivalve shells; those with a nacreous layer of mother-of-pearl are most efficient because of their shine, which helps to attract more fish. Shells discarded after their contents had been eaten must have been adapted as tools; they are hard enough for many tasks, and their use would have conserved more valuable metals.

The Phoenicians used murex shells for purple dye, but it is not known whether the art was also practiced further south on the Arabian Peninsula. The chief source of ink in the ancient world of the Mediterranean was *Sepia*, the cuttlefish. Although the inks used today are mainly synthetic, the cuttlefish bone is still used as a source of calcium for birds and as a polishing ingredient in toothpaste. "Silk" woven from the byssus of the giant *Pinna* shell, which is found in both of Saudi Arabia's bordering seas, was used to knit gloves in Italy as late as the 19th Century and may have been the "golden fleece" sought by the legendary Greek, Jason.

An exquisite example of mother-of-
pearl inlay (*tarsia*) from Syria.
(*Kit Constable-Maxwell*)

A handsome antique necklace of Gulf pearls, shown arranged on several valves of black-lipped pearl (*Pinctada margaritifera*). (*Kit Constable-Maxwell*)

Shells have been used both as a medium for measurement and for exchange over many centuries. Money cowries (*Cypraea moneta*) were first used in this fashion by the Egyptians; since these particular cowries are not found in the Mediterranean, they must have come from the Red Sea where they were available. (The first metal coins used by the Chinese in 600 B.C. were, in fact, shaped like small cowries.) Although the use of cowries for money has continued up to the present century in Africa (the value increasing in direct proportion to distance from the source), there is no record of cowries (or shells of any sort) being used as money in the Arabian Peninsula.

Coral colonies are made of a crystalline form of calcium carbonate and thus have the same chemical composition as limestone. This "coral rock," which often also contains large quantities of molluscan material, was quarried from the exposed reefs on the shores of the Red Sea, and used in Jeddah as building blocks. Semi-fossilized shells can be seen in the exterior walls of some of the city's picturesque 19th Century houses. There is some evidence that lime was burned by early shore dwellers; the beach rock used for this operation being also largely composed of semi-fossilized marine shells, is easily broken down into gypsum, the main material used in the manufacture of cement, which is now a large industry in Jeddah.

Cowries and pearls have been used in jewellery since ancient times.

Early neolithic inhabitants of what is now Jordan arranged *Dentalium* shells in diadems or caps, some of the finest of which were buried with their dead. One necklace found in a tomb at Jarwan, in the eastern region of Saudi Arabia dates circa 100 A.D. and includes two small gold beads shaped like cowrie shells and several pearls. Small cowries and triangular medallions of mother-of-pearl have also been used to decorate the apparel of some of the Arabian Peninsula's more recent inhabitants. Mother-of-pearl shell was used for ornaments in Egypt as early as the 6th Dynasty (c. 3200 B.C.). Nacre is a more technical name for this iridescent lining deposited by the mantle on the inside of a large group of shells, including tops, turbans, oysters, and mussels, although the largest and most workable quantities come from the pearl oyster (*Pinctada margaritifera*). It can be sawn into slabs and ground down without destroying its iridescence; the surface can become "blind," however or lose its iridescence, possibly following prolonged exposure to the sun.

No one knows when the art of pearl-shell carving began in the Middle East, but its peak was reached by the time of Ur of the Chaldes (2500 B.C.), after which it disappeared (perhaps when ivory became the favored material). By the 7th millenium B.C., shell carving had become a specialized art. At Baidha, an important center on the trade routes from the Arabian Peninsula to the Jordan Valley and the Mediterranean coast, a complete bazaar of shell-carving workshops was found. In the Gulf large conch shells were later used as raw material along with the pearl shells. Pearl-shell carving continued to flourish, but, when the Islamic conquerors put an end to the use of figurative design in Moslem countries after the 6th Century A.D., it took the form of geometric and abstract designs. Mother-of-pearl inlay in furniture (*tarsia*) had apparently been carried on in Damascus since Sumerian times, and it was either from there or from Egypt that it was introduced into 16th Century Palestine, where an important school began to flourish. One important factor that contributed to the intensity of pearl-shell carving is its hardness and, hence, its durability. Most materials used to decorate musical instruments are considered to have some beneficial effect to their tone, and one theory holds that nacre contributed to resonance. For this reason, mother-of-pearl is still widely used as inlay on Middle Eastern musical instruments.

Both mother-of-pearl and pearls (*lulu* in Arabic) have symbolized purity and beauty in the Middle East since ancient times. Pearls are the only gems perfected by nature and requiring no application of skill by man to enhance their beauty. Those of the best gem-quality come from the black-lipped pearl oyster (*Pinctada margaritifera*); a slightly lesser quality is found in the golden-lipped pearl oyster (*Pinctada maxima*), which is more often fished for its mother-of-pearl lined shell. A natural pearl is produced by chance when a small piece of sand or debris enters the shell and lodges in the mantle. The mantle's reaction to this irritation is to smother it in nacre, producing a pearl. More often, however, the foreign body lodges between the mantle and the shell; in this case, the mantle cements the foreign body against the inner surface of the shell, the result being a blister pearl. The mantle of nearly every kind of shelled mollusc is capable of producing a hard coating around an irritating body. The resulting "pearl" will, however, have the same appearance as the shell's inner surface; the pearl will be nacreous only if the inner shell is as well. For example, one giant clam (*Tridacna*) can produce a golfball-sized "pearl" in 10 years, but it will be covered with the same dull white shell as the inside of this clam.

The ancient pearl fisheries were principally in the Gulf, on the coasts of Ceylon and India, and in the Red Sea. Pearls were distributed among the nations controlling the fisheries, and other people received collections from them either as presents, in conquest, or by trade. Considering the very large accumulations that must have existed, relatively few pearls of antiquity now exist, and these are of no great ornamental value. Those now remaining in archaeological collections and art museums have more or less decayed through the ravages of time and the accidents to which they have been subjected; since they are organic substances rather than minerals, they could not survive being buried for thousands of years in relatively moist soil.

Assyrian bas-reliefs show sovereigns and great personages of those countries adorned profusely with pearls, not only in their jewellery but also on their garments and even in their beards. Representations of ancient Egyptian costume do not seem to show pearls being used as decoration to any great extent, but Egyptian women did have pearls in their jewellery as early as 1500 B.C., and the wealthy commonly possessed both marine pearls from the Gulf and freshwater pearls from the Nile.

By the 5th Century B.C., Red Sea merchants were travelling to Hang-chow and other northern ports in China with pearls and mother-of-pearl shells. The Chinese, who used pearls as medicine, searched their own waters for pearls and later succeeded in establishing, at least in one place, moderate pearl fisheries.

Greek and Roman literature referred to an extensive pearl industry in the Gulf more than 2,000 years ago. The Greek philosopher Appolonius of Rhodes described how he thought that the pearl fishermen of the Arabian Gulf made cultured pearls. First, he said, they rendered the sea smooth by flooding it with oil (hardly necessary, considering the usual calm days there). Then they dived into the sea and held out small containers of the aromatic herb, myrrh, as bait to induce the oyster to gape. Quickly, they inserted a low hollow pin into the opening and drew off the pearl-making liquid, which was then placed in iron molds to solidify. Ptolemy speaks of the pearl fisheries that had existed from time immemorial at Tylos, the Roman name for what is now the island of Bahrain.

Massoudi, one of the earliest Arabian geographers, noted the existence of Gulf pearls in the 9th Century, and Ibn Batuta, the physician-traveller from Tangiers, wrote about them in 1336 A.D. The Gulf was almost the only important source for pearls throughout the 18th Century. In 1838, its fisheries employed 4,300 boats manned by more than 30,000 men. Of these, 3,500 boats were from Bahrain alone, mostly 1 to 50 tons each with 3 to 15 men aboard. Although pearling was carried on at will all year long, June through September were the preferred months. The Arab pearl diver was able to bring up 10 to 12 oysters per dive, and to make 30 to 40 dives per day of five to six minutes' duration. Although there are oyster reefs throughout the Gulf, they occur in the greatest abundance on the Arabian side. In 1908, the pearl banks were located from a few hundred meters to 96 kilometers offshore, but, by 1941, workers had to travel almost double that distance to find them. By 1930, it was estimated that pearls from the Gulf, which are predominately light yellow with a soft nacreous luster, supply seven-eighths of the world's production.

The Red Sea, although not of great importance in the total numerical production of pearls, was one of the most ancient sources, especially during the reign of the Ptolemies in Egypt. As early as the 3rd Century B.C., Nearchus said that "in the Red Sea lies an island where precious pearls are found." Whiter than either Gulf or Ceylon pearls and with a stronger luster, Red Sea pearls occur most extensively among the Dahlak Islands and the Farasan Islands in the southern part of the Red Sea. The pearling operations in both the Gulf and Red Sea were often financed by Indian traders, who furnished capital for equipment and purchased the pearls in gross lots. Consequently, these pearls were usually marketed in Bombay and Madras. Only a small number of the Gulf pearls were sold in Bahrain itself and those from the Red Sea were not reported in the official returns of the Red Sea ports. It is difficult, therefore, even to estimate the quantities taken.

In this century, two Japanese pioneered the production of cultured pearls, and another entrepreneur made a business of selling cultured pearls. Suddenly, the bottom dropped out of the natural pearl market. Cultured pearls are usually harvested after their second or third years of growth, 40 per cent of the "crop" having market value (although fewer than 10 per cent are of gem quality). Natural and cultured pearls can usually be differentiated by X ray, as the 2 to 7 millimeter freshwater shell bead inserted to start the cultured pearl will show up as being larger than the particle of sand or sediment that began the natural pearl. Otherwise, both types develop exactly the same way. It is only the difficulties involved in their collection and their rarity that keep the price of natural pearls high.

The relationships between man and molluscs are many. Shells have been used as food, tools and decoration, as we have seen. They have also been used for medicinal purposes in the past, for early man used everything at some time for treatment, often because of shape alone. The cowrie, for example, has been used as a symbol of fertility for thousands of years. More recently, some marine clams have yielded possible anti-viral and anti-carcinogenic substances; other scientists are investigating the control of the freshwater snails that carry parasitic diseases fatal to man.

As much as man used shells for treatment, he occasionally needed treatment because of them as well. Cone shells are poisonous, although relatively few deaths have been directly attributed to them. Infective hepatitis can result from eating infected bivalves; more rarely, paralytic shellfish poisoning, which can be fatal, may occur. Molluscs cause damage to man in other ways. Perhaps the most infamous of shells is the *Teredo* shipworm, which is not really a worm at all but a burrowing bivalve that consumes the wood of ships' hulls and jetties and used to be a major cause of loss among wooden ships.

Edible molluscs are a good source of protein and will be of greater importance in the future when the potential of mariculture is more fully realized (although increased pollution could adversely affect the development of this relatively new industry).

Molluscs are an excellent barometer of sea conditions; an absence of certain types of molluscs is a good indication that pollution or other abnormal environmental conditions exist. There is no way to measure and predict the exact effect of sewage on the delicate organisms of the sea, but species will, in fact, decrease and die off in a systematic order indicative of the severity of the environmental changes.

Environmental upsets affecting the natural balance can take many forms. Oil spills of more than 4,500 liters are especially destructive to bivalves because their microscopic breathing and feeding cilia are paralyzed by the oil that eventually sinks to the bottom. Introduction of foreign molluscs can be a form of pollution, because, if an animal has no natural enemies in the new environment to keep it in check, it can well become a pest by eventually destroying the useful native species.

A new and serious threat to the open expanses of salt marshes, which are often sources of nutrients for offshore fisheries and nursery ground

Two Arab children's games are played with cowries (*Cypraea*). Four lynx cowries (*C. lynx*) are used in a throwing game. Dice used in a game similar to Parcheesi are cut gold-ringers (*C. annulus*). (*Kit Constable-Maxwell*)

To announce the happy tidings of a marriage, one tribe of bedouin puts this cloth decorated with cowries (Cypraea), *Marginella*, and triangles of mother-of-pearl on a post in front of the bride's domicile.
(*Kit Constable-Maxwell*)

Where they are

for billions of mussels, snails, crustacea, and fishes, is the thermal pollution from desalination plants. A rise in sea temperature of only a few degrees, especially in summer, could turn these marshes into potential deserts. Of equally serious impact in the Red Sea is the effect of municipal and domestic waste and sewage disposal, especially in lagoons behind the fringing reefs. These semi-enclosed areas rapidly accumulate noxious agents and lack the means to flush them out. Natural causes periodically kill off great numbers of molluscs, as well. Exceptionally low tides can expose vast expanses of reef to a fatal drying.

Some damage to the reef is caused by those who come to admire its beauty. Thoughtlessly, they pick up pretty seashells, only to discard them when they begin to decay and smell, not being interested enough to have learned that they contain living animals. There is no need for even a serious shell collector to take more than a few specimens of a particular shell; it is far more acceptable and, indeed, challenging for collectors to photograph the living animals. The resulting pictures are more interesting, for one then sees and begins to appreciate the beauty of the soft parts of these animals, which, in many cases, equals or even surpasses that of the shell alone.

Legislation establishing marine reserves and prohibiting coral and shell collecting within those areas has already been enacted for some parts of the Red Sea. It is hoped that such controls will be introduced throughout most of the region before too long, for the reefs are living laboratories, and they and their inhabitants are of great educational and scientific value. Not only do their related ecosystems play a critical role in potential fisheries schemes, but they also demand protection in their own right as beautiful national treasures. They are susceptible to man's interference and need to be managed correctly for his benefit as well as for his enjoyment.

SHELL PROVINCES

In the mid-19th Century, S. P. Woodward, who studied the distribution patterns of mollusc, distinguished and named 14 principal shell provinces in the world. A province is defined as an area in which at least half of the species inhabit only that region, although some species can invade the waters of neighboring provinces. They may be adjoining but are usually at least partially separated by barriers such as land masses, ocean currents, and differences in salinity and water temperature; the last two of these are especially important.

The Indo-Pacific Province, the largest, warmest, and richest shell province in the world is notable for its abundance of colorful shells and strange and unique molluscs. Characterized by the presence of coral reefs, it extends from the eastern coast of Africa through northern Australia to eastern Polynesia and from Hawaii through the Far East and southeast Asia to Arabia. Because this province is so vast, it has been subdivided into Australia, the Hawaiian chain, the Philippines, the Red Sea, and the Arabian Gulf. The Red Sea and Arabian Gulf are isolated warm-water pockets off the Arabian Sea noted for their many unique subspecies.

ZONES OF THE SEA

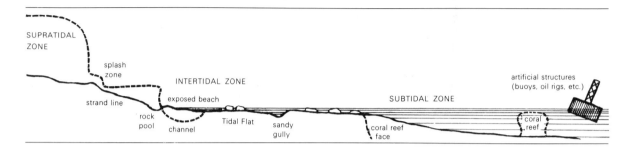

SUPRATIDAL ZONE

splash zone

INTERTIDAL ZONE

artificial structures (buoys, oil rigs, etc.)

strand line

exposed beach

SUBTIDAL ZONE

rock pool

channel

Tidal Flat

sandy gully

coral reef face

coral reef

Seas cover about 72 per cent of the Earth's surface and are, with their shores, divided into zones determined by their location and the nature of their bottoms. These zones plus other factors such as the availability of food, tides, wave action, and water temperature make up the habitat and determine which shells will live in an area.

Supratidal zone

The splash zone is an area that lies between the highest point of ordinary tides and that of extraordinary storm tides. Although the few molluscs that might be tossed up this far during a storm offer good shelling for the collector, the splash zone is not normally a habitat of marine molluscs.

Intertidal zone

The seashore (littoral) is a boundary strip between the land and the sea. Its living conditions are highly variable, as it is both bleached by the sun and washed by the sea. Also called the intertidal zone, this area lies between the uppermost part of the land that is directly affected by the tides and the lowest area exposed at low tide. The two types of area within the intertidal zone are (1) exposed beaches of sand or rock, which can have special features such as rocky pools, and (2) tidal flats and creeks with muddy, sandy, or rocky bottoms.

Exposed beaches

The dominant feature of these beaches is their exposure to the direct sun; the upper edge of the intertidal zone may be submerged only during one or two of the highest tides each lunar month. Sand beaches are generally steeper than lower areas and are composed of unconsolidated sand and pebbles, often mixed with broken shells. Wave action causes size sorting; because heavier pebbles do not travel as far as lighter shells, it is often possible to find empty shells of the lighter weight varieties

thrown up near the "strandline," the level of the high tide, which is often marked with a line of seaweed.

Intertidal rocky areas can vary from beaches of smooth pebbles and rocks to rough coralline cliffs and often have tidal pools like marine gardens. In temperate climates with daily tides, these rocks and pools provide a stable and well-inhabited environment for intertidal species.

Tidal flats

The second type of littoral or intertidal zone includes tidal flats with muddy, sandy, or rocky bottoms. The outstanding feature of these areas is their low relief, which results in very poor drainage. Water movements affect sedimentation; coarser sediments are deposited in areas of greater water movement, whereas finer particles remain suspended and settle down later in the quiet ebb and flow of more gentle water movement. It is for this reason that beaches on the open coast consist of pebbles, shell fragments, and coarse sand and that mud flats are found in sheltered bays.

Tidal flats are known to be among the most productive of natural ecosystems, and mud flats are especially productive because excess organic matter accumulates in the sediment. Stands of mangrove trees may be found in mud flats near the shore.

Sand flats are found where the wave energy is greater than in the mud flats but still less than on exposed beaches. Rippled by the ebbing tide, these sand flats are often grayish in color, owing partly to their content of organic matter. The grains of sand in this area are finer than those on the beaches and may, in fact, be only a thin layer overlying a rocky or beach-rock substratum.

Rocky tidal flats are found in gulfs and bays where conditions favor the formation of beach rock. This type of flat may be found also in sheltered sections of the open coast, but the texture of the rocky bottom of the coastal flats is rougher than that on the bottom of bays.

Subtidal zone

The subtidal (sublittoral) zone of the sea is found below the lowest tide level and includes environments with soft bottoms, hard bottoms, or no associated bottom.

Soft bottoms

The various types of soft bottoms may be difficult to differentiate between because they can merge imperceptibly. They include muddy, sandy, or grassbed bottoms, and their sediment can vary from coarse coral gravel to fine shell-fragment sand, to silty sand, or to mud with or without sand or clay.

As in the intertidal zone, mud bottoms generally occur in low-energy areas. Because their fine particles are tightly packed, circulation is poor, and the oxygen penetrates the sediment slowly. Consequently, the level of organic breakdown is low, and there is an excess of unoxidized organic matter.

Sandy-bottomed areas, similar to their intertidal counterparts, are formed and maintained in high-energy environments having vigorous water movement caused by either wave action or currents. Their bottom is usually porous and has good circulation, oxygen, and nutrients. Sandy subtidal bottoms are found in the zone immediately below exposed sandy beaches and in deeper offshore waters in the vicinity of coral reefs and islands.

Turflike areas of grassbed grow rooted in sand, silt, or mud and trap silt and organic detritus from the overlying water. The substratum is eventually built up to a point where the grassbed is actually slightly elevated. Grassbeds occur at depths of about 1 to 15 metres depending on the availability of light and the clarity of the water and are highly productive environments.

Hard bottoms

Hard-bottomed environments include a somewhat surprising trio of rocky bottoms, coral reefs, and artificial structures.

Hard rock bottoms often occur as subtidal extensions of flat intertidal *faroush* platforms. They can be either smooth or rough, and the rougher sort may support a heavy growth of algae. Their most outstanding feature is one of regular joints and fissures. Where they extend from limestone cliffs, there is often a shaded 1-to-2-meter-wide channel immediately under the cliff that is slightly deeper and cooler than the boulder-strewn reef flat farther out. Sand-filled gullies about 20 centimeters deep and up to 2 meters wide can be found on the rocky reef flats; in coves, these gullies of sand may be replaced by a continuous cover of sand over the reef rock. Rocky bottoms can occur anywhere from the beach to depths of 15 meters or more and are also found underneath corals.

Coral reefs, the second type of hard bottom, are the most productive of all marine environments in terms of both energy and rate of production of new organic matter. Corals are sometimes solitary animals, but almost all reef-building corals grow in colonies composed of enormous numbers of individual polyps, joined together in a continuous sheet of living tissue and supported by a stony, dead, calcareous skeleton of complex architecture having a characteristic structure for each particular species. What are usually seen are the skeletons of the massive, rounded, solid corals, because, when the branched corals die, their skeletons are broken up into rubble, worn down into sand, or occasionally even cemented together by the growth of other coral or coralline algae.

Coral's environment must meet specific requirements in order for it to exist. Clean water is necessary because more than a minimum of sediment will clog the corals' tentacles and prevent breathing and feeding. Coral requires temperatures of at least 18° to 20°C. The photosynthetic algae that endow the reef-forming corals with the ability to deposit their limestone skeletons rapidly, require a continual supply of sunlight, which penetrates seawater sufficiently to a maximum depth of 100 meters and thus confines corals within this limit.

The ecology of a coral reef is extremely complex. In opposition to factors encouraging the developing of coral reefs are other factors that limit development and sometimes work to break it down. Calcium carbonate, of which coral rock is made, dissolves slowly in seawater, and wave action wears it away. Some molluscs bore into the coral reef; fish eat or bite at it; and some molluscs scrape away the surface layer.

Manmade structures such as ports and navigational aids and oil-producing platforms of steel, concrete and wood, harbor dense, complex communities of organisms and quickly become "artificial reefs." Although such a colony's species are often typical of hard bottoms, they constitute a distinct mixture of species, because the structures on which they grow offer a combination of environmental conditions different from that of any naturally occurring environment. The resulting mixture of species is drawn from several different types of intertidal and subtidal environments. Manmade structures are ecologically important because they offer scientists an excellent opportunity to study depth zonation.

The open sea

In addition to intertidal and subtidal zones associated with different types of bottoms is the habitat of the open sea. Although it has the largest single area of any zone (85 per cent of the sea is deeper than 2,000 meters), perhaps only 100 species of mollusc live as pelagic adults near the surface of the ocean, some floating and others being attached to sargassum weed or merely hovering in mid-water.

Two small tibias (*Tibia* sp.) from the Red Sea—Red Sea specimens. (*Kit Constable-Maxwell*)

3 Molluscs of Saudi Arabia

Arabian habitats

If the nature lover wanders much on shores or other localities where molluscs are to be found, he cannot help noticing how their lives and habits are associated with their surroundings and with the other animals living there.

The molluscs found in various habitats differ greatly, and, although some of their special characteristics enable them to live in a particular place, others have developed in response to their environments. The study of the relationships of organisms with their surroundings and with one another is called ecology, and it is one of the most fascinating aspects of the natural history of the seashore. Most marine molluscs live on the continental shelves and in coral reefs from the low-tide line to depths of approximately 100 meters, the majority being found above 30 meters.

SUPRATIDAL HABITATS

The cliff tops and areas of beach above or beyond any moistening spray from the sea and subjected to the high temperatures and relentless sun of the coastal regions of Saudi Arabia are usually devoid of molluscan life.

INTERTIDAL HABITATS
EXPOSED BEACHES

Exposed beaches extend from the supratidal zone through the splash zone and into those intertidal areas having either muddy, sandy, or rocky bottoms. When the sandy beach is subject to drying, either because of its high location or because of the sun and wind, its sand can reach temperatures of 70°C, which will kill most animals. If the sandy beach is further down in the intertidal zone, where it remains damp, it will stay somewhat cooler, but the minimal water circulation during low tide will bring little oxygen to buried and burrowing organisms. When the waves of the occasional high tides move large amounts of sand in or out, organisms in this area must move rapidly to avoid being either washed away or buried too deeply. They must also be able to protect themselves against the abrasive action of sand stirred up in the surf. The dominant molluscs in this habitat are gastropods, almost all of which burrow into the sand when the tide is out.

Exposed rocky beaches in temperate climates are usually stable, highly productive environments. The abundant rocks normally provide firm

Left: The club-spined murex (*Homalocantha anatomica*) averages only 4.5 centimeters and lives in coral rubble—Red Sea specimen. (*Kit Constable-Maxwell*)

59

Above: The open sea from the top of the 20 meter limestone cliff in Al Wajh. (*Gunnar Bemert*)

An intertidal sandy beach along the Red Sea. (*Gunnar Bemert*)

attachment for large algae and seaweed, which, in turn, provide food and shelter for the inhabitants. The rocky beaches of Saudi Arabia generally lack a covering of large seaweeds, since the hot sun prevents its growth above the low-tide mark, but rocks and cliffs in the intertidal zone on both Saudi Arabian coasts are often blackened in areas by other small algae.

The molluscs of exposed rocky beaches and cliffs are usually zoned in a horizontal band determined by environmental conditions. For example, many rock-dwelling snails make daily migrations at night either to search for food or to follow the wet intertidal zone. Species most resistant to drying and to extremes of temperature are found near the high-water mark; those species colonizing the intertidal rocks have developed various methods of attachment in order to withstand the waves and strong currents that threaten them. Often, the rocks around a tidal pool are fissured by corrosion and wave action, and crevices full of sand and organic debris become habitats for bivalves. Deeper crevices may contain some seaweed, which is food for many gastropods, especially winkles, tops, whelks, and dog whelks.

The inhabitants of tidal pools are determined by the sizes and positions of the pools in the intertidal zone, for the conditions will be similar to those of the rocky beach or cliff but more exaggerated. If a pool is shallow and exposed to the sun, whatever its position, it becomes overheated and does not support a rich community. If it is well flushed with seawater, it may contain a balanced community of predatory molluscs (such as dog whelks), scavengers (some Buccinidae whelks), and herbivorous molluscs (winkles and limpets). If it is lower on the shore and deep, it may provide an intertidal refuge even for subtidal species such as chitons, limpets, mussels, and tops.

TIDAL FLATS

In muddy tidal flats, especially mangrove swamps, one finds a greater variety of invertebrate life dependent upon the decay of falling leaves for food. Relatively few species are found in the muddy waters of mangrove tidal flats, but the populations of those that do occur are enormous. The roots of mangrove trees offer anchorage and shelter to oysters and other bivalves, which, in turn, provide food for predatory gastropods. Seaward of the mangrove belt may be a zone of algal mat inhabited by many small gastropods.

If there are patches of very loose, wet, coarse-grained sand near the low-tide level in the mud flats, there will be a variety of larger burrowing animals. The water movements of these areas are important, especially the waves of varying intensity, because an animal that can withstand the waves will find an increased amount of nutrients on a wave-beaten shore.

In beach-rock flats of corallized limestone, or *fasht* that are frequently uncovered by low tide, most of the animal life is found in cracks between sheets of stone or under loose blocks, because the sediment of coarse shell sand and silty mud under them is usually anaerobic. The animals in these cracks will be the same ecological types as those found on a rocky beach. In areas of the fringing reef that are seldom completely uncovered by the tide and where there are loose or broken coral boulders, it is often possible to find migrants from the subtidal coral reefs.

SUBTIDAL HABITATS

Two major factors affect all organisms occupying the subtidal habitat. The first is the physical nature of the seabed (soft or hard bottomed); the second is the depth, which controls the amount of light received and the intensity of water movement. The physical nature of the bottom on or in which organisms live is important, because there are great differences in the adaptations required by animals living in hard and rocky areas and by those inhabiting soft or sedimentary areas. Plant forms used as food by molluscs are most abundant in shallow water near the coasts; the sunlight and the mixing of these inshore waters by waves and tides are good for the growth of free-floating plankton and anchored algae, which

A stand of mangrove trees south of Al Wajh. (*Gunnar Bemert*)

61

An intertidal reef flat with a mixture of sand and rock. (*David Harris*)

provide nourishment for molluscs. Consequently, these areas also often serve as nurseries.

SOFT BOTTOMS

Mud-bottom inhabitants must contend with reduced oxygen circulation among the fine, close-packed particles of their substrate and so must either live in the thin oxygenated surface layer or develop special adaptive mechanisms for obtaining oxygen or enduring its lack. Because the need for mobility is less in fine-grained mud flats, many inhabitants of this area burrow. For these burrowers in soft bottoms, the size of sediment grains becomes a major factor.

The variety of species living in soft-bottomed environments with sand as the substrate also depends on the grain size and stability (or mobility) of the sand. Sand-bottom dwellers must be more agile in order to live in their high-energy environment with its constantly shifting sand. They also benefit from good supplies of oxygen and nutrients in well-circulated water. Light penetration is also important to inhabitants of this area. Relatively clear water will, for example, enable microalgae to form a photosynthetic film on the sand grains to a depth of about 10 meters to provide food for the inhabitants.

Habitat also affects the shape of a shell. Sandy shores and seabeds are the ideal areas for burrowers and harbor many gastropods, most bivalves, and nearly all the tusk shells. Sand-dwelling gastropods usually appear in one of two shapes. The first group is essentially spherical but has a large, broad, shovel-like foot for ploughing through the sand or across its surface. The other inhabitants of sandy areas have long and slender shells, like the augers. Because a tapered shape encounters less resistance when it moves through the sand, shells in the second group have a relatively small wedge-shaped foot and long siphons so that they can burrow deeper and feed to better effect. Where the sand is mixed with mud, the molluscan fauna is even richer, and shells are often larger and even more perfectly shaped.

Grassbeds are considered here as a third type of soft-bottomed habitat, because, although they are rooted in mud, silt, or sand, the grass gives them an added dimension and enables a different sort of habitat to develop. Although they occur in the sea, they are not seaweeds but are, in fact, flowering plants related to pondweeds which create areas resembling fields of grass. The so-called grassbeds trap silt and organic detritus from the water and slowly elevate them above their own substratum.

HARD BOTTOMS

The substrates of hard-bottomed habitats include various mixtures of rough and smooth rock, coral, and manmade artificial structures. Patches of rough and fragmented rock may occur offshore from rocky exposed beaches to great depths and may contain varying amounts of coral debris. Their many crevices, niches, and projections offer ample room for shelter for many hole and crevice dwellers. Creeping snails, which are often grazers, find ample supplies of algae here, and predatory gastropods hide in the crevices. Many sessile molluscs (often bivalves) squeeze between the rocks and exhibit a great variety of methods of attachment. Cemented to a rock by one valve are the oysters (*Ostrea*), jingle shells (*Anomia*), and jewel boxes (*Chama*); arc shells (*Arca* and *Barbatia*), mussels (*Mytilus*), and pearl oysters (*Pinctada*) are attached by bundles of byssus threads,

An inhabitant of shallow sandy waters, the heavy *Tibia insulaechorab insulaechorab* is endemic to the Red Sea. (*Kit Constable-Maxwell*)

which they can dissolve to release themselves. Hammer oysters (*Malleus* and *Isognomon*) live wedged into crevices or under rocks, whereas date mussels (*Botula* and *Lithophaga*) bore into soft rock.

Coral reefs are the second type of hard-bottomed habitat. Some molluscs are directly associated with the living corals of the reef. Less mobile species bore into the living corals or lie embedded in or attached to them. Although they are seldom seen, there are a few types of mollusc either on or inside the soft corals, the horny corals, and gorgonians. If one looks at a stem of coral, one discovers many small inhabitants. In areas of maximum diversity (the central Pacific and western Indian Oceans), thousands of species are estimated to inhabit a coral reef, exhibiting an intricacy of adaptation and ecological specialization rivaled on land only by tropical rain forests.

The richest and most varied population of molluscs is not found on the reef itself but in the coral rubble adjacent to living corals. On the sheltered side of a reef, broken coral is eroded by wave action, and patches of coral sand accumulate. This type of area is often especially rich in

Underside of coral boulder showing a *Cryptopecten pallium*—Red Sea specimen. (*Kit Constable-Maxwell*)

Right: In the moist area of the cliff overhang, red nerites (Nerita) and small grey *Nodilittorina milligrana* and *Planaxis sulcatus* secure themselves in small niches. *Planaxis* have siphonal canals, which *Nodilittorina* lack—Red Sea specimens. (*Kit Constable-Maxwell*)

Above: On rocky intertidal shores, small tent-like limpets (Patellidae) called *Cellana eucosmia* are found stuck tightly to the rocks—Red Sea specimens. (*Kit Constable-Maxwell*)

Above right: Several similarly-shaped sand-dwellers. From left to right, back row: *Casmaria ponderosa*, *Malea pomum*, and *Bulla ampulla*. Front: *Natica onca*, surrounded by five small *Natica gaultieriana* with *Polinices tumidus* on the right—Red Sea specimens. (*Kit Constable-Maxwell*)

(Photographs on page 68–88 are all Red Sea specimens.)

molluscs such as carnivorous cones (*Conus*), augers (*Terebra*), and miters (*Mitra*), which feed on worms and bivalves; occasionally scavengers such as olives (*Oliva*) feed on dead fish and crabs. Indeed, one cup of shelly sand taken near a coral reef may contain more than 60 species of microscopic mollusc. Although a small reef the size of an average living room may be the ecological habitat of hundreds of fishes representing several dozen genera and species, a square meter of the same reef will often contain invertebrates in such abundance that it surpasses the fish population of the entire reef.

Artificial structures constitute the third type of hard-bottomed habitat. In some instances, species in this zone appear in greater abundance than they do in their normal rock or coral habitats (for example, on metal structures), because many other hard-bottomed boring species are absent. One interesting trait of these "artificial" communities is that they show a well-defined ecological succession (that is, they change in an orderly way with time). In general, each succeeding community will show a greater diversity of species, greater individual size, and a greater community area.

THE OPEN SEA

The third type of subtidal habitat is the open sea; about 30 families, or 200 species, of floating mollusc spend their entire lives in the open seas. In addition, most species spend a short span, at some point during their veliger stage, somewhere at sea between the surface and 8 kilometers down and later regularly rely on the open sea's plankton to nourish them, but, other than some cephalopods, few live any of their adult life as pelagic species.

Red Sea molluscs

Other than works in technical journals beyond the reach or interest of the layman with only a casual interest in shells, there is relatively little literature on the molluscs of the Red Sea. In the last two decades, Cousteau, Roessler and, most recently, Bemert and Ormond have published popular books about the Red Sea and its inhabitants, but none of these mentions molluscs more than briefly.

Most of the many thousands of species of mollusc in the Red Sea fall into four classes—Gastropoda (the snails and slugs), Bivalvia (the clams and oysters), Cephalopoda (the octopus, squid, and cuttlefish), and chitons (Polyplacophora) which only occur in scattered localities. The greatest number are, by far, in the first two classes. Little information is available on cephalopods, so they will be mentioned only briefly. There are few tusk shells (Scaphopoda) in the Red Sea and they will not be discussed.

INTERTIDAL MOLLUSCS
EXPOSED BEACHES

There are many intertidal sandy beaches on the Red Sea coast of Saudi Arabia. Those known best by the author are in the north near Al Wajh; a few island beaches northwest of Jeddah are also sandy, but most sandy beaches are inland of extensive reef flats and are supratidal. Where an intertidal sandy beach remains moist while the tide is out, ceriths (*Cerithium*), necklace shells (*Natica*), olives (*Oliva*), moon snails (*Polinices*), and *Nassarius* may burrow.

The exposed rocky beaches of the Red Sea coast consist of raised cliffs of limestone in which occasional fossilized molluscs and coral colonies can be seen. These cliffs separate the coastal plain from the reef shelf nearly the length of the coast and are rich in rocky pools. Here and there, they are interrupted by sandy coves and long stretches of sandy beach. In the Al Wajh area, the winter and spring storms occasionally spray the tops of the 20-meter cliffs. This northern area experiences a limited daily tide and thus has some molluscs that do not occur near Jeddah; for example, a 5-centimeter long chiton (*Acanthopleura haddoni*) is found in abundance in rocky areas at or below the tidal level. Periwinkles (Littorinidae) are also seen in large numbers in the cracks and crevices of the rocky shores and tidal pools of Al Wajh.

The cliff tops near Jeddah are devoid of gastropods, for there is almost no tide to moisten them and few crevices for shelter. Erosion, however, has left a 1- to 2-meter overhang that creates a perpetually damp and shaded area harboring varied molluscs. This area has a 25-centimeter-wide zone of *Planaxis sulcatus* (Superfamily Cerithiacea) at its outer edge. A few periwinkles, such as *Nodilittorina millegrana* and *N. subnodosa*, can be found scattered in the damp overhang, but it is inhabited primarily by the ridged slipper winkle *Nerita undata*. Below, where the cliff face becomes vertical, nerites such as the spirally-banded *N. albicilla* and the smooth, multicolored *N. polita* extend up from the water line and about a meter out onto the reef flat.

Clockwise, from the upper right:
Conus monachus, C. pennaceus, C. arenatus, C. striatellus; the small *C. taeniatus, C. nussatella,* and *C. distans.*
(*Kit Constable-Maxwell*)

TIDAL FLATS

Mud-bottomed environments are not frequent in the Red Sea, but they occur occasionally in still lagoons and mangrove areas. South of Al Wajh, there are intermittent stands of mangroves growing at the back of bays and creeks in shallow salt-water flats with bottoms of stagnating sediments. Although these intertidal mud flats have high temperatures and salinities, they can be extremely productive. Coastal waters are, however, much more productive.

The fringing reefs of the Saudi Arabian coastline are broken by occasional sandy coves and lagoons. These quiet, low-energy areas may accumulate deeper layers of sand and various mixtures of sand and silty mud.

Oliva bulbosa is one of the relatively few species of olive (Olividae) found in the Red Sea. Olives remain hidden in fine sand during the day and become active at night. They are predators, so carnivorous that they can be captured on a baited line. Necklace shells (Naticidae: *Natica* and *Polinices*) have an extremely large foot that enables them to move, bulldozerlike, through intertidal or subtidal sand. Helmet or bonnet shells (Cassidae: *Cassis, Phalium,* and *Casmaria*), are larger sand dwellers that feed on sea urchins, and sand dollars. They have heavy and solidly built shells, often with sculptured knobs or other protruberances; the lip is also thick, usually with prominent teeth.

Bulla ampulla, the bubble shell (Bullidae), is not uncommon in the Red Sea. It is an intermediate form of opisthobranch in which a small, thin shell is retained. In life, the shell is partially covered by the edge of the mantle. From the top, the live animal looks almost like a fried egg, as it is usually seen ploughing through the surface layer of fine sand. *Bulla ampulla* browses on algae; other members of this order are predators feeding on foraminiferans (single-celled organisms), worms, and bivalves.

The cuttlefish (*Sepia*) is usually seen in sandy areas and lagoons, swimming with undulating movements of the mantle around the edge of its body. *Loligo* sp. is a beautifully colored squid found close to the sandy bottom.

The cones (Conidae) are usually confined to shallow tropical waters but have diversified to occupy a variety of habitats including intertidal sand and rock flats; some, however, live on sandy bottoms at depths of more than 60 meters. One of the most common cones on intertidal sandy bottoms is *Conus arenatus*, which is white and speckled·with tiny brown dots that tend to form two or three dark bands. In sandy bays, *C. achatinius* (designated by J. G. Walls as *C. monachus*), *C. lividus, C. quercinus,* and *C. sumatrensis* (designated by Walls as *C. vexillum*) can be found. The orange-spotted *C. tesselatus* has been found in such widely diverse habitats as muddy mangroves and shallow rocky waters.

The patterns on cones vary greatly even within a single species. This variation makes the classification of cones confusing; for example, mainland specimens are often much darker than those found on a reef. It is sometimes difficult to see a cone's true pattern, for often the periostracum is thick and brown and obliterates the shell's design. One example, commonly known as the virgin cone (*C. virgo*), is probably the largest

A member of the triton family,
Distorsio anus prefers shallow sandy
bottoms. (*Kit Constable-Maxwell*)

A member of the Cymatiidae family, the hairy triton (*Cymatium pileare* is shown here with its proboscis extended, eating the black-edged mantle of a scallop (Pectinidae). (*Kit Constable-Maxwell*)

and heaviest cone to be found in the Red Sea. Its periostracum hides a dull, pale yellow, almost matt surface above a purple tip.

There are three subdivisions of cones, grouped according to their prey; numerous species are predators of worms, others eat molluscs, and a few types eat small fishes. The radula of these carnivorous hunters has been reduced to a series of separate, detachable, elongated darts with barbed pointed tips, held one at a time in the proboscis (although 20 are stored in the radular sac). The proboscis containing the radula is capable of sudden extensions to a length almost equal to the shell's own, and the dart is shot into the prey.

Associated with the radula is a large salivary gland modified to produce poison along with every dart. This poison is specific and in the species of cone that prey on vertebrates is extremely poisonous to man. Great care should be taken in handling all cones; the pointed end should never be touched, as it is the canal for both the siphon and the proboscis. A cone should not be laid on the hand as the proboscis can bend to inject an object below it. The common tented cones (*C. textile*, *C. omaria*, and *C. pennaceus*) fall into this dangerous category, as does the extremely toxic striated cone (*C. striatus*), very commonly found in the Red Sea.

The Red Sea coastline is often a relatively flat reef rock platform 90 meters to 1 kilometer wide with both intertidal and subtidal areas. This flat substratum has many sand-filled depressions about 20 centimeters deep and 2 meters in diameter and is covered in other places with a continuous layer of sand of varying depths. Although the inner reef flat may be exposed at low tide, the sandy gullies remain subtidal; however, they may like the rocky pools in the intertidal area, become overheated and supersaline at such times.

These reef flats are characterized by a lack of daily tide and by a relatively large seasonal fluctuation in temperature. Instead of daily tides, water-level variations of as much as 0.75 meter can occur from strong onshore or offshore winds lasting up to two weeks. These winds also cause extremes of temperature which are low enough in winter to result in molluscan mortalities and high enough in summer to cause a migration of the intertidal reef flat's inhabitants toward the subtidal reef crest in search of cooler waters. Because of these two factors, the intertidal and adjacent subtidal reef flat in Jeddah is characterized by molluscs that, in cooler environments, occupy only the rocky intertidal zone. For example, R. N. Hughes found *Morula granulata*, a muricid, high up on intertidal rocks in the colder winter months, but it migrated to a subtidal area in September.

Members of the predatory triton family (Cymatiidae) are both sand- and rock-dwellers and often inhabit the intertidal zone. Species more commonly found in shallow Red Sea waters are the small *Distorsio anus* (in

Above: The heavy vase shell, *Vasum turbinellum* lives in shallow water on a variety of substrates and feeds on marine worms. (*Kit Constable-Maxwell*)

Right: Related to the slender augers of shallow sandy beaches, the heavy marlin spike (*Terebra maculata*) is found in deeper waters in coral-sand bottoms among the coral reefs. (*Kit Constable-Maxwell*)

71

sand), the hairy triton (*Cymatium pileare*) and tiny red *C. rubecula* (in coral and rocks). The *Distorsio* eat worms found in the sand and *Cymatium* eat smaller gastropods and bivalves. Their far relatives, the frog shells (Bursidae) are also intertidal rock dwellers, but differ by having two apertural canals instead of one. Red Sea species include *Bursa* sp. and *B. granularis*.

The tulip, band, or spindle shell family (Fasciolariidae) generally lives under coral rocks intertidally and is represented by the moderately large brown *Fasciolaria* (*F. trapezium* and *F. filamentosa*) and *Latirus* (*L. turritus* and *L. smaragdulus*). The thin and elegant genus *Fusinus* (represented by *F. leptorhynchus*), however, lives on a subtidal sand and coral rubble bottom at a depth of more than 4 meters.

SUBTIDAL MOLLUSCS

On the shores of shallow sandy lagoons or bays, the round and mobile Venus clam (Veneridae: *Gafrarium pectinatum*) is found just below the surf. The surf clams (Mactridae), and tellins (Tellinidae) burrow deeply and therefore have slightly elongated, smooth, thin shells and are notable for their long siphons. The augers (Teribridae) are long, narrow, many-whorled shells tapering to a very sharp point. Several found in abundance in the subtidal sandy beaches south of Al Wajh and in fewer numbers near Jeddah are *Terebra dimidiata*, *T. crenulata*, and *T. sublata*. There are not many species of tibia (Strombidae) found in southern Asia, and two are found in muddy or silty quiet areas of the Red Sea; the Arabian tibia (*Tibia insulaechorab insulaechorab*) and *T. insulaechorab curta* are found in shallow waters, the latter more commonly in the extreme south of the Red Sea.

Grassbeds are not a common biotope on the eastern coast of the Red Sea as the conditions are not conducive to their growth. Conditions such as active deeper waters with little sediment favor the development of coral reefs.

One hard-bottomed area of the inner reef flat at the base of the rocky cliff always remains subtidal. This 1- to 2-meter-wide channel is deeper than the seaward reef flat; the water here is shaded until midafternoon and, in summer, provides a cool refuge for species occupying the rocky intertidal zone. A mixture of shells commonly found on the adjacent reef flat extends into this channel. The vase shell (*Vasum turbinellus*) is fairly common but takes shelter during the day under dead coral rocks. Although the algal growth is poor, a small chiton (*Acanthochitona* sp.) can be found here on rocky surfaces, in company with the muricid, *Cronia margariticola*. Hughes reported *Octopus* c.f. *cyaneus* using the channels under the cliffs near Jeddah for courtship at the end of February.

Small octopus are also occasionally seen among the rocks in the shallow waters of the reef flat; the most common of these is *Octopus macropus*. Some species of mollusc seem to occur on the inner reef flat in zones; for example, the inshore whelk *Engina mendicaria* is replaced beyond 35 meters by *Columbella testudinaria*. The mussel *Modiolus auriculatus* is dense 1 to 4 meters from the cliff, thins out over the sandy inner reef, and becomes abundant again in the breaker zone. Inhabiting sandy patches

A cephalopod, related to the cuttlefish and squid, the *Octopus* prefers the bottom, only swimming in an emergency. (*Gunnar Bemert*)

Right: The common top shell (*Tectus dentatus*), showing the contrast between the alga-covered shell and the animal's colorful foot. (*I. Sharabati*)

Lower right: Another common top shell, the little 1- to 2-centimeter strawberry top (*Clanculus pharaonis*) grazes in clusters. (*I. Sharabati*)

and pockets are three small strombs: the pink-mouthed white *Strombus gibberulus albus*, the mottled brown and white *S. mutabilis*, and the brown-striped endemic Red Sea species, *S. fasciatus*. Horn shells or ceriths (Cerithiidae) are also abundant in the sandy patches on the reef flats. Actively creeping and burrowing within the surface layer of sand to feed by grazing on plant material, they are characterized by a great variety of sizes, colors and designs.

Loose, dead coral boulders up to 1 meter in diameter are scattered on the reef flat. Murexes (Muricidae) are commonly found around these

The large Arab dhow and its smaller dugouts, traditionally used to hunt the nacre-lined top shells. (*Angie Pridgen*)

boulders. In some, the radula has been adapted to drill holes through shells such as barnacles and bivalves, on which these carnivors feed. In order to subdue their prey, murexes often inject them with a paralytic substance "purpurin," which was the Tyrian purple that became famous as the dye used to color the imperial cloaks of the Roman emperors. Murexes can be difficult to identify because the sculpturing of the shell, determined by environmental conditions, is often marred by abrasions and marine growths. In the Red Sea, the murex *Chicoreus ramosus* is characterized by frilly ornamentation. The drupes (Thaididae), which are closely related to the murexes, inhabit a variety of subtidal bottoms: under rocks in tidal pools, in sand at the low-tide line, or under coral on the algae-coated reef face at depths of 5 meters. Some species, such as *Drupa lobata* and *D. morum morum*, prefer wave-swept reefs and strong surf.

The topshells (Trochidae), are distinguished by a top shape, a horny operculum in a rounded aperture, and a nacre-lined interior. Tops tend to inhabit rocky areas in tidal pools, subtidal reef flats, and the tops of reefs at sea. *Tectus dentatus*, which is of commercial interest, is common in the Red Sea. In its 6 years of life, this top shell grows up to 8 centimeters and forms an especially thick lining of mother-of-pearl, which was collected and cut for shirt buttons at the turn of the century. Although these top shells are common on the inner reef flats, fishing was traditionally on reefs at sea from small dugout canoes carried there by Arab dhows. The large dhows were anchored, and men paddled the dugouts from reef to reef searching for the top shells with glass-bottomed tins. Another Red Sea species is the tall red and white *Trochus maculatus.*

Turbans (Turbinidae) are another family in the superfamily (Trochacea). They are often found in tidal pools close inshore or where the water is more active on barrier reefs at sea. Instead of the horny, slightly flexible operculum of the top shells, the turban's operculum is thick, round, and calcareous. It is often colored to look like a cat's eye, perhaps as a defence mechanism to frighten away marine predators. The shells of the tapestry turban (*Turbo petholatus*) are beautifully smooth and glossy and are called *Abu Imma* or "father of the turban" in Arabic. *T. argyrostomus* is a rigid, rough-shelled variety of turban more commonly found whole on the inner reef flats or reef tops. The tapestry turban is more fragile and often survives only in tantalizingly beautiful fragments.

Perhaps the most popular shells in the world are the glossy cowries (Cypraeidae). Many species of cowrie inhabit intertidal or immediately subtidal areas and live among broken corals for protection. Little is known about the cowrie diet: many seem to be nocturnal herbivores, feeding on algae that they scrape from the substrate with their radula; others graze on sponges; a few seem to be entirely carnivorous. When a cowrie is alive, its mantle is usually extended up over the outside of its shell, enveloping and protecting it fully, which is why it stays shiny and lustrous. The mantle may be thin and translucent, or thick, with a color pattern very different from that of the shell. The mantles of some species possess innumerable papillae and act as camouflage and possibly a supplementary respiratory organ.

A cowrie grows rapidly, reaching its maximum size in two to three months. The outermost layer of the shell with its characteristic pattern is formed last; to increase its size, the animal must thereafter dissolve part of the inner strata of its shell. As the shell matures, its apex disappears, the last whorl encloses the earlier smaller parts of the spire, and the thickened outer lip rolls into a toothed edge. Cowries do not have an operculum, perhaps because the elongated shape of the aperture makes the fitting of an operculum difficult. The foot does, however, protrude from the aperture.

Other molluscs of the offshore reefs occur in zones matching the shore and reef flats already discussed. Thus, sand dwellers, which like the turbulent waters of the outer edge of the fringing reef, will be found on the windward side of a patch reef at sea and, likewise, sand dwellers of the reef flat will be found in sandy pockets in reefs at sea.

Many species of cone are found where the water is more turbulent. The dangerous geography cone (*Conus geographus*), lives in hiding in the sand, under coral clusters, and comes out at night moving rapidly in the hunting of small fish.

The predatory tritons (Cymatiidae) inhabit sandy bottoms in deeper waters, usually near coral reefs. The most famous is the large Triton's trumpet (*Charonia tritonis*) which divers would be wise to leave in place, for they feed on the reef-destroying Crown-of-Thorns and are therefore of crucial importance in maintaining the ecological balance of the reef. *C. tritonis* manages the delicate task of feeding, by holding this poisonous starfish down with its foot, penetrating the spiny skin with its radula, and scraping out the inside of the Crown-of-Thorns through this single wound, leaving an empty sac.

The strongly-ribbed harp shells (Harpidae) are related to the volutes of the Indo-Pacific. Although they were well represented in the early Tertiary period, they now number fewer than twelve world species. *Harpa amouretta* lives very deep in the sand of shallow areas on the reef; frequently found dead on beaches in Al Wajh, it is rarely seen alive. *H. major* and *H. ventricosa* are also present in the Red Sea but dwell in deeper waters.

A larger group of sand-dwellers, the strombs (Strombidae), are also commonly called conchs, a word which may lead to confusion, because the romance languages use variations of it to mean any shell. All strombs have conspicuous, highly colored, stalked eyes and a characteristic deep notch at the anterior edge of the outer lip through which one eye stalk normally protrudes. A large species of stromb, locally called a "finger conch" (*Lambis truncata sebae*) is found on subtidal sandy bottoms near coral reefs. All herbivores, the strombs feed on algae and organic debris in the shallow sand in which they live. In many tropical areas, the large conchs are eaten and are rapidly disappearing as a result of overfishing, but this problem does not seem to have appeared yet on the eastern shores of the Red Sea. Perhaps the most unusual genus of Strombidae is the *Terebellum terebellum*. There seems to be only a single species of this small, fast-moving shell, which catapults itself along in sand and over the reefs and flats.

Another group of carnivorous sand dwellers, the thin-shelled tuns (Tonnidae) are not particularly numerous and prefer sand in deeper water

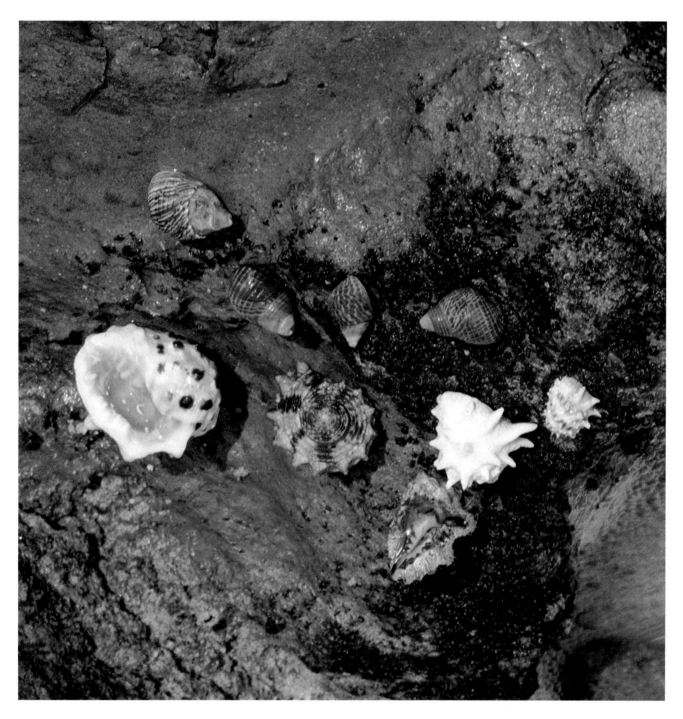

Several rock-dwelling species of
mollusc are shown against a coral rock
cliff.
Top: Four brown periwinkles
(*Littorina*)
Middle right: Two *Drupa ricinus*
Center: top view of a *Turbo
argyrostomus*
Left: a lavender-mouthed *Drupa
morum morum*
Bottom: the dark and frilled *D. lobata*
(*Kit Constable-Maxwell*)

Above: The carnelian cowrie (*Cypraea carneola*) has a lilac tint at the base and aperture and violet-stained teeth. It is unusual in its feeding habits, for it feeds during the day. (*Gunnar Bemert*)

Top left: Some cowries live in pairs, but the spotted lynx (*Cypraea lynx*) lives in swarms. (*I. Sharabati*)

Lower left: The stolid cowrie (*Cypraea stolida*) has a transluscent and pale mantle. (*D. Sharabati*)

Top: Difficult to distinguish from the *Cypraea arabica* cowrie, the *C. grayana* is more commonly found in the Red Sea. (*I. Sharabati*)

Above: Another endemic Red Sea
cowrie is the camel cowrie (*Cypraea
camelopardalis*). (*I. Sharabati*)

Top left: The Red Sea's endemic red-
spotted cowrie (*Cypraea erythraeensis*)
was at first thought to be rare, but this
opinion may be revised when the
home colony is discovered.
(*D. Sharabati*)

Middle left: The cowrie, *Cypraea
cayrica*. (*I. Sharabati*)

Above: An endemic Red Sea cowrie,
the panther cowrie (*Cypraea pantherina*)
is abundant and often confused with
the tiger cowrie (*C. tigris*) which has a
similar, almost infinite range of color
variations. Although common in the
Indo-Pacific, *C. tigris* has been
collected only rarely in the
southwestern part of the Red Sea and
not at all near Jeddah. (*I. Sharabati*)

Right: The geography cone (*Conus geographus*) is a large lightweight cone with a very wide aperture, to accommodate the ingestion of small fishes. (*I. Sharabati*)

Lower right: The Triton's trumpet (*Charonia tritonis*) showing the color-coordination of animal and shell. (*I. Sharabati*)

beyond the reef's edge; these fragile shells are seldom seen except as broken pieces on the shore. The grinning tun (*Malea pomum*) is the most common tun in the Red Sea; the partridge tun (*Tonna perdix*) is only an occasional "find."

The large (up to 30 centimeters) bivalve pen shell (*Pinna muricata*) is shaped like a giant mussel and is usually buried upright with its rounded end above the mud or sand substratum around corals. Its pointed end is attached by its byssus deep in the mud to stones or pieces of hard substrate. The projecting edge seems to get broken regularly, but the animal can withdraw into the remaining portion of the shell and quickly repair the damage. The closely related *Pinna bicolor* and *Atrina vexillum* are also found in the Red Sea in similar habitats.

The family miter shells has been separated by recent research into two families (Mitridae and Volutomitidae). Many miters are sand dwellers, but some inhabit a variety of other biotopes, including coral rubble and the living reef. Over a dozen varieties have been reported from the Red Sea, and three specimens of *Mitra mitra*, not previously reported from the Red Sea, have been collected from coral sand bottoms at a depth of 15 meters.

Some species of mollusc prefer areas of living coral, whether it is on the reef face of a fringing reef or a patch reef at sea. Conspicuous here are the gaping clams (Tridacidae), which settle between opposing heads or branches of coral and allow themselves to be engulfed. *Tridacna maxima*, usually brilliantly colored, excavates a shallow depression in which it sits, always tightly attached by a stout byssus. The giant clams "farm" zooxanthellae, which not only supplement but may replace their original

A group of small strombs. Clockwise: 4 various colors of *Strombus terebellatus*, an orange-mouthed *S. fasciatus*, 3 various colors of *S. mutabilis*, the cylindrical *Terebellum terrebellum*, the wide-flanged *S. plicatus columba*, the fingered *Aporrhais pespelicani*, 2 pink-mouthed *S. gibberulus albus*, showing some color variation, and a brown-striped endemic *S. fasciatus*.
Center: *S. bulla*. (*Kit Constable-Maxwell*)

Strombus tricornis, has an elongated main whorl and a single narrow flare that makes it easily identifiable. (*Kit Constable-Maxwell*)

food source by filter feeding. *T. squamosa* is a deeply-frilled version that lives attached by a weak byssus in coral rubble. Other bivalves attach themselves by byssus threads to dead, lower parts of branches of large, bushy corals or the undersides of massive corals. In the same habitat, the scallop (Pectinidae) can be seen moving about freely on its own.

Some bivalves bore into the coral rather than tying or cementing themselves to it. The mussels (Mytilidae), include several species called date mussels (*Lithophaga* sp.) because of their color and shape. All members of this group live in rounded, tubelike borings (up to twice the length of the shell itself) in which they are attached by two sets of byssus threads; by contracting them in different ways, the mussel can rock by pulling on either set. This rocking may help scrape away material from the end of the boring (which is already paste-like because of an acid

Above: The large mussel-shaped
Atrina vexillum, or pen shell.
(*Kit Constable-Maxwell*)

Right: The mantle of *A. vexillum* is a
distinctive black and white stripe.
(*I. Sharabati*)

secretion from its mantle). Most of these shells bore into dead rock, which may become grown over again with live coral; the animal must then bore outward to retain its distance from the entrance as the live coral thickens. Another family of boring clams includes the flask shells (Gastrochaenidae), recognized by their entrances, which are built up by calcareous secretions into two flask-shaped tubes used as inhalant and exhalant siphons.

Among the bivalves that cement one of their valves to the corals, the thorny oyster (*Spondylus gaederopus*) is conspicuous because it is usually covered with a bright red sponge. It prefers deeper water and is usually found below 10 meters, where it may be cemented on the lower lobe of a *Porites* head, but it is more often found beneath overhangs. In similar locations and just as conspicuous because of a covering of red sponge are the zigzag-edged valves of the cockscomb oyster (*Lopha cristagalli*), which is itself a dull purple color. Also cemented to the corals are the true oysters (*Ostrea*) and the jewel boxes (*Chama*), the latter being characterized by a thick, rough shell, the uppermost valve of which is smaller and fits on top like a lid.

Members of the family Vermetidae (a mesogastropod) rarely attract much attention, as their shells look like worm casts in the coralline rock. One, *Dendropoma maxima*, is both abundant and conspicuous, ranging from the flat, rocky reef crests down to a depth of 1 meter, where there is moderate current and wave action. The *Dendropoma*'s 2-centimeter circular hole in *Porites* coral is blocked at its entrance by a horny disc, and when the *Dendropoma* dies, small fish such as blennies often take up residence in these shell-lined tubes.

Although the subclass Opisthobranchia, or sea slugs, is not as varied as the shelled snails, there are at least several dozen species living in and around the coral reefs in the Red Sea. They are not infrequently found by divers but are much less well-known by the general public, perhaps

Above: The cockscomb oyster (*Lopha cristagalli*) is a purple color, but this example is also covered by red sponge. (*Gunnar Bemert*)

Opposite page: The thorny oysters (Spondylus) nearly always have a covering of red sponge. (*I. Sharabati*)

because it is virtually impossible to preserve them. The only possible way to enjoy their beauty after the initial underwater encounter is to photograph them and leave them behind in the sea. All sea slugs should be handled with care, however, as their secretions can cause inflammation and blistering of human skin.

The largest order of opisthobranchs to be found in the Red Sea, and also one of the most attractive group of sea slugs, is called Nudibranchia or "naked gills." They are characterized by a variety of delicate filamentous appendages to their mantles. There are five or six fairly common species, all brightly colored and feeding on sponges. Many are 1 to 2 centimeters long, although they can vary from the size of a grain of sand to large species weighing up to 1.5 kilograms.

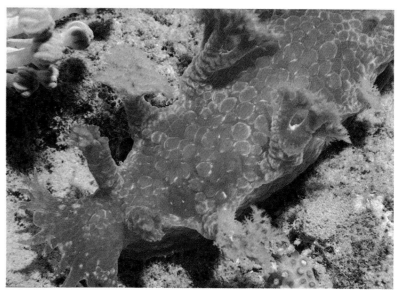

Above: *Marionia* sp. A lovely and
fluffy pink nudibranch. (*I. Sharabati*)

Above left: *Pteraeolidia* cf. *semperi*, one
of the small dragon-shaped aeolids, has
typically-clustered cerata in which
stinging cells from ingested prey are
stored. (*Gunnar Bemert*)

Top: *Chromodoris pulchella* is a
nudibranch of the dorid group, which
is characterized by a central tuft of
secondary gills near the end of the
mantle. (*Angie Pridgen*)

Left: The orange and white *Gymnodoris striata* has an unusual fan-shaped gill on its back. (*I. Sharabati*)

Lower left: The *Halgerda willeyi* is a rubbery black, white and yellow nudibranch. (*Gunnar Bemert*)

Below: *Phyllidia* are characterized by warty protuberances on their back. Three colorful examples: this clown-like *Phyllidia* sp. (*Gunnar Bemert*)

Bottom left: . . . *P. varicosa* (*Tom Blackerby*)

Bottom right: *Phyllidia* sp. (*Gunnar Bemert*)

Right: *Dendropoma maximum* "fishes" with sticky threads of mucous material which, with the help of wave action, can extend up to 8 centimeters from the aperture to trap floating plant material. Every 10 to 15 minutes, the mollusc hauls in its "catch", swallows both the net and its contents, then secretes a new net and begins "fishing" again. (*Gunnar Bemert*)

Opposite page: Several local species of bivalve are arranged on a tide-cut Gulf beach:
Back row, left to right: a pair of *Trachycardium leucostoma, Periglypta reticulata, Cucullaea labiata* (Arcidae), a white *Andara* cf. *antiquata* (Arcidae), and *Chlamys ruschenbergerii* (Pectenidae). Front row, left to right: two *Trachycardium flavum*, an unusually pink *Nodipecten nodosus*, and two unidentified Veneriidae. In the front are four *Cardita antiquata*.
(*Kit Constable-Maxwell*)

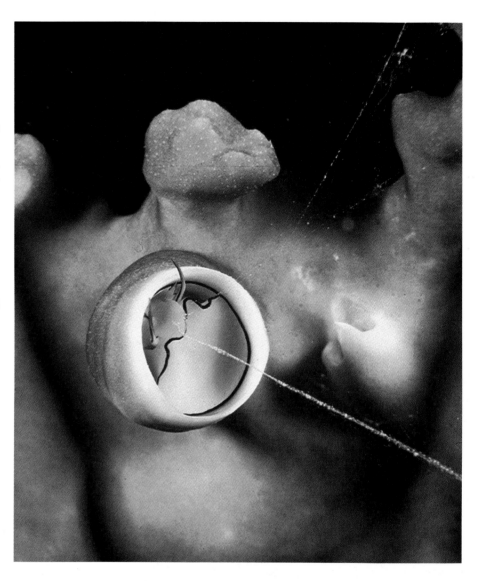

One sub-order, (Aeolidacea), carry rows of pointed filaments along either side of their mantle, either elliptically shaped or grouped in clusters called cerata, which have been adapted to aid in the animals' defence. The aeolids typically feed on anemones and hydroids and are apparently able to ingest nematocysts (stinging cells). These cells are digested whole and passed by outgrowths of the liver to the cerata, where they are stored until an attack, at which time they are ejected through a pore in the end of the cerata. When they come into contact with seawater, the stinging threads are activated in the predator's face.

Another sub-order, Doridacea, contains rather flattened forms of nudi-branchs. Many dorids carry a tight rosette of tufted secondary gills near the end of the middle of the mantle.

Other dorides, the Phyllidiidae are characterized by wart-like pro-truberances on their backs.

The members of another order, (*Aplysimorphia*), which can occasionally be seen in the Red Sea, are commonly called sea hares because they have a pair of long upright tentacles on their elongated heads. The largest living opisthobranchs, their foot has prominent parapodial lobes that it uses for creeping or swimming. Sea hares inhabit shallow coastal waters, where they live and feed on large algae that they cut off with their well-developed radula.

Artificial structures, primarily piers and navigational aids, are not yet numerous in the Red Sea. These manmade environments are ecologically much like hard-bottomed habitats and will probably be found in future studies to contain much the same mixture of inhabitants.

Arabian Gulf molluscs

In the Arabian Gulf, little has been recorded about the molluscs of the Saudi Arabian coast. H. E. J. Biggs and L. L. Grantier and, more recently, K. Smythe have studied the molluscs of this area, and a large study carried out by Basson and others for ARAMCO included the molluscan inhabitants of this environment.

INTERTIDAL MOLLUSCS

The prevailing northerly wind in the Gulf blows at an acute angle to the coast, and the surf also strikes at this angle. Because of the low relief of the Saudi Arabian Gulf coastline, the wind-blown sand is redeposited to the southeast. Such sand movement has a major influence on coastal landforms; long hook-shaped sand spits are often seen running southeast from major headlands or coastal projections; there is a large proportion of beach, and an unusually extensive intertidal zone. Sand-rich areas with pockets of sand between and under patches of sand-scoured rock are

found on exposed beaches in the lower half of the intertidal zone. The white carbonate sand on these beaches is finer grained than that found elsewhere and is of organic origin. It has some grains of terrestrial quartz, often colored red or yellow by a coating of iron oxide.

EXPOSED BEACHES

High exposed beaches of rock are not common on the Saudi Arabian coast of the Gulf. In those which do exist, the rock surface is subjected at low tide to extreme heat and dessication by the sun and a good establishment of algae is prevented, although a blue-green variety noted for its resistance to adverse environmental conditions appears as a dark blackish color on some intertidal rocks along the shores, either forming a mat on the surface or boring into the outermost rock layer. Without an abundant algal shelter, the most successful molluscs are those that inhabit crevices, holes, and the underside of boulders or those that are mobile (vagile) and are capable of retreating into these shelters. Heavily built, thick-shelled species that are able to cling firmly to the rocks are also among the rocky beach dwellers. For example, the carnivorous dog whelks (*Thais* and *Cronia margariticola*) feed on the barnacles and bivalves that inhabit this area. Herbivorous gastropods found grazing on the limited algae on rock beaches include the turbans and tops, such as *Lunella coronatus* and *Trochus erythraeus*. Small periwinkles (*Nodilittorina subnodosa*) share their habitat under rocks, in gravel and coral rubble near or above the high-water mark, with the equally small and similar *Planaxis sulcatus* (Superfamily Cerithiacea). The related ceriths (*Cerithium*) prefer sandy substrates, and so are usually found in sandy pockets among the rocks, feeding on diatoms and plant detritus.

TIDAL FLATS

The tidal flats of the Saudi Arabian Gulf coast are an important intertidal area totalling between 500 and 1,000 square kilometers and usually having mud or very fine sand bottoms. Their width is usually greater than 1 kilometer, and, in many Gulf bays, they account for 30 to 40 per cent of the total area, often on the sheltered southeastern side of major headlands, an excellent example being Tarut Bay.

There are extensive tidal mud flats on the Arabian Gulf coast, especially on the sheltered southeastern sides of projecting headlands.

In its study of Gulf biotopes, ARAMCO has sub-divided the tidal mud flat into several zones on the basis of the dominant lifeforms contained in each. Few molluscs appear in the marsh grass through mangrove zones, but the seaward algal mat zone hosts populations of ceriths and associated species. Beyond the next very wet, liquid-mud area, at the level of the lowest possible tide, is the area called the *Cerithidea* zone (dominated by the species *Cerithidea cingulata* which occurs here in populations of up to 2,100 per square meter). In the same zone are the carnivorous and predatory *Murex kusterianus*, *Nassarius* and *Fusus* (both Superfamily Buccinacea), and the horn shells (*Pirenella*) and the related *Planaxis* (both Superfamily Cerithiacea). The seemingly omnipresent

Inhabitants of exposed rocky beaches:
Top: The herbivorous rock-dwelling
turban *Lunella coronatus*. Middle: The
carnivorous drupe *Cronia margariticola*.
Bottom: The grazing top shell
Monodonta canalifera.
(*Kit Constable-Maxwell*)

bivalve *Gafrarium* occurs in this zone as well as nearly all others, along
with the hammer oysters (*Malleus*).

The most uncommon type of tidal flat in the Arabian Gulf, and also
the least productive, is that with a sandy bottom. However, where the
sand is loose, wet, and coarse near the low-tide mark, a few species of
bivalves can be found (*Arca, Cardium, Gafrarium, Mactra,* and *Tellina*).
The more numerous species of gastropod are similar to those found in
sandy beach habitats: ceriths (*Cerithium*), dog whelks (*Nassarius*), necklace shells (*Natica*), *Strombus, Murex* and *Bulla*. K. Smythe has recently

studied the incidence of several *Tornatina* (Superfamily Bullacea) in the fine algae in shell sand, at the same time discovering and naming a new genus (*Retusa tarutana*) from Tarut Bay. Some species of *Tellina*, surf clams (*Mactra*), and Venus clams (*Gafrarium*) are also found here, but there are only about half as many species of bivalve as gastropod in this area.

The rock-bottomed tidal flat zone occurs especially in hypersaline bays and along sheltered areas of open coast. There are extensive areas of *faroush* or tidal rock in flat, seamed sheets 10 to 20 centimeters thick, which for centuries was systematically harvested from Tarut Bay for building stone.

In the Gulf, the variety of molluscan species in rock flats seems to be greater than that in any other littoral zone. The species are the same types found on the rocky beach or subtidally under loose sheetrock and are also found in this zone either under the rock or in the cracks. The bivalves include the Venus clams (*Circe* and *Gafrarium*), arc shells (*Arca* and *Barbatia*), cockles (*Cardium*), oysters (*Crassotraea*), jewel boxes (*Chama*), scallops (*Chlamys*), pearl oysters (*Pinctada* and *Isognomon*), the related hammer oysters (*Malleus*), mussels (*Lithophaga*), pen shells (*Pinna*), and thorny oysters (*Spondylus*). Gastropods which occur in nearly equal numbers include *Cerithium* and the related *Planaxis*, dog whelks (*Cronia* and *Thais*), periwinkles (*Nodilittorina*), tops (*Trochus* and *Monodonta*), turbans (*Turbo*), and margin shells (*Marginella*).

SUBTIDAL MOLLUSCS
SOFT BOTTOMS

Of the three types of soft-bottomed subtidal habitats, mud bottoms and grassbeds occur in more areas of the Gulf than do sand bottoms. Mud bottoms are often found offshore from tidal mud flats, and, below 30 meters, most of the Gulf is mud-bottomed.

At depths of from 6 to 25 meters, small filter-feeding cockles (*Cardium papyraceum*) usually occur, partly buried in the mud, in densities of 5 to 10 (and sometimes as many as 50) per square meter. Other shells often seen in sandy-bottomed habitats can also live in mud. These include the bubble shells (*Atys*, *Bulla*, and *Retusa*), ceriths (*Cerithium* and related *Rhinoclavis*), *Cronia*, *Murex*, necklace shells (*Natica*), tops and turbans (*Trochus* and *Turbo*), turrids (Turridae), carrier shells (*Xenophora*), the predatory wentletraps (Epitoniidae) and miters (Mitridae) among the gastropods, and arc shells (*Arca*), scallops (*Chlamys*), sunset shells (Gari), pearl oysters (*Pinctada*), pen shells (*Pinna*) and *Tellina* among the bivalves.

Some subtidal sand-dwelling molluscs prefer calm waters similar to those found in lagoons. The cerith-shaped *Pirenella*, which usually prefer muddy bottoms where they feed on detritus, have been recorded in sandy-bottomed areas of the Gulf. The long and slender screw shells (*Turritella*) like this fine sand in which they also search for plant detritus. The grazing turbans and topshells (*Turbo* and *Trochus*), can be found on sandy bottoms and in the loose sand are the bivalves *Arca*, *Cardium*, *Cardita*, *Gari*, *Tellina*, *Chama*, *Pinctada*, and *Pinna*. Although the carrier shell (*Xenophora*) has been recorded in this habitat by ARAMCO, it is

A *Lima* bivalve, which is capable of
swimming. (A small red sea squirt
like a flower beside it.) (*Gunnar Bemert*)

Pinctada radiata. This pearl oyster averages 6.5 cm. in diameter, is brownish-yellow with radial rows of purplish patches, and is elliptical to ovate with large unequal ears and concentric scaly ridges. (*Kit Constable-Maxwell*)

usually a deep-water species. Some carnivorous species which usually inhabit the shallower intertidal sand-bottomed habitats can also be found subtidally: the whelks (*Thais, Cronia* and related *Morula*), bubble shells (*Atys*), olives (*Oliva* and the related *Ancilla*), moon snails (*Natica*), *Murex, Nassarius*, and cones (*Conus*), which eat not only worms and other molluscs but also fish.

A second distinct type of sandy-bottom community lives in areas swept by a strong current of up to 2 knots, which creates sharp-crested 3- to 4-meter-long dunelike ridges of coarse sand at right angles to the axis of the current. This movement of water causes a rapidly shifting surface layer of extremely unstable coarse-grained sand in which few species can survive, but dense populations of small clams called *Ervilia scaliola*, measuring only a few millimeters long, can live in this restricted zone. These troughs often contain grassbeds, the third type of subtidal soft-bottomed habitat.

One of the most important and extensive habitats in the Arabian Gulf, grassbeds provide homes for numerous fish and invertebrates, some of which feed directly on the grasses; other inhabitants depend directly or indirectly on the grasses for food made available through its decay. In a sample taken from grassbeds, an ARAMCO survey identified 165 species of burrowing molluscs or molluscs with specific adaptations to the grass. The interlacing leaves shelter vulnerable young commercial shrimps and also furnish attachment sites for young pearl oysters (*Pinctada margaritifera* and *P. radiata*). These bivalves live by attaching themselves with byssus threads; unlike the firmly attached true oysters, however, they can release these threads in order to move to another location (although at a rate of only a few centimeters per day). Their life cycles are synchronized to match the growth cycles of the grassbed, and their main "spatfall" (when the new larva settle in) is in the late spring. Hundreds of oysters are attached to each blade of grass, where they remain throughout the summer and grow to lengths of about 5 millimeters. During this period, they are difficult to see, even where they are thick enough to overlap like shingles, for they are the same green as the grass. By October, the grass begins to die and come adrift, and the small oysters must turn themselves loose, crowding onto the remaining blades in patches so dense that they can be seen from the air as blackish areas in the sea. As the grass continues to die, the oysters move down the slope and re-attach themselves to more solid substrates, the result being dense beds wherever there is a suitable hard substrate just seaward of a grassbed.

Bubble shells (*Bulla ampulla*) and the predatory margin shells (Marginellidae) crawl in or under the detritus layer; the carnivorous *Murex kusterianus* is usually seen half buried often holding a clam on which it is feeding. The filter-feeding pen shells (*Pinna*), near relatives of the pearl oyster, grow up to 40 centimeters long. Other bivalves burrow under the top layer of sand, the date mussels (*Lithophaga*) attached by a byssus and the unattached Venus clams (*Gafrarium*). Two members of the class Cephalopoda (*Octopus* and *Sepia*) can also sometimes be seen in the waters of shallow subtidal grassbeds.

Single areas can contain various types of zones and can be remarkable for the different varieties and numbers of species found in them. In the later 1950's, Biggs and Grantier enumerated the molluscs of Ras Tanura, a fingerlike spit running 10 kilometers out into the Gulf on the eastern side of Tarut Bay. Most of the shells listed were found by Grantier on the bay side of the spit, where the bottom is mostly sandy with a few areas of rock. Of the 32 types of gastropods found, the largest groups of species were *Cerithium* and *Murex* (4 types each) and *Cypraea*, *Strombus*, *Nassarius*, *Thais*, *Turbo*, and *Siphonaria* (2 types each). Single examples of *Trochus*, *Nerita*, *Xenophora*, *Natica*, *Drupa*, *Oliva*, and *Conus* were recorded. In the same area, Grantier also found 32 different types of bivalves. In contrast, on the Gulf side of the spit, where the shore is paralleled by a reef and deepens sharply, live shells were found only in the few areas where the beach is rocky and shallow. The hardy blue-green algae colonizes these small subtidal rocks and even the shells of sand-dwelling molluscus such as the conch *Strombus decorus persicus*.

HARD BOTTOMS

The rocky type of subtidal hard bottom is usually found either as a subtidal extension of beach rock (*faroush*) or in low-activity, high-salinity bay areas in the Gulf.

On shallow subtidal rocks, one finds such mobile animals as chitons, limpets, and herbivorous snails which graze on the dense cover of small algae; the predatory *Thais savignyi* prey on other molluscs or barnacles.

One variety of large cockscomb oyster, *Hyotissa hyotis* has tubular processes on its outer surfaces.
(*Kit Constable-Maxwell*)

Above right: *Cypraea esontropia*. Three of these cowries were recently found feeding on sponges in the Gulf.
(*Kit Constable-Maxwell*)

Left: A small species of cockscomb oyster (*Lopha folium*) which attaches itself to branches of black coral by a few recurved spines on its upper surface is shown next to a large winged pearl oyster (*Pteria penguin*).
(*Kit Constable-Maxwell*)

Below a depth of 3 meters are other areas containing a type of flat, smooth rock plate, which may be many meters across and often exhibits a network of joints and fissures but does not harbor many animals, except around its crevices. The maximum depth of the rocky bottom in the Gulf is usually 12 to 15 meters, and, when it is silt covered, it too may support dense colonies of pearl oysters (*Pinctada*). Cowries such as *Cypraea turdus* and other snails such as *Cerithium, Trochus, Thais, Murex,* and *Drupa* also favor rocky bottoms. Many bivalves such as thorny oysters (Spondylus) are seen permanently attached to the exteriors of rocks in this zone. The sessile hammer oysters (*Malleus*) and pearl oysters (*Isognomon*) are found in crevices, and date mussels (*Lithophaga*) can be seen boring into rocks.

It is perhaps because the Gulf's vast shallow subtidal areas are silty that its coral growth does not rival that of the Red Sea, in spite of its equal sunshine. The coral reefs that do exist contain several specific and often very different habitats, which are often mixtures of other types of zones.

On the innermost sand flat of the reef, numerous sand dwellers such as small conchs (*Strombus decorus persicus*) mate and lay their eggs in summer. Seaward, the sand is coarser and extensively burrowed by invertebrates. The cones are well represented on the reef, especially the *Conus textile* and *C. vexillum*. Other shells found in and around the coral reef include *Drupa, Cerithium, Morula, Strombus, Thais, Trochus, Turbo,* and *Nassarius*. Many colorful varieties of nudibranchs are also seen in the reef environment and the massive, smooth corals called *Porites* are inhabited by several species of boring bivalves. The coral reef is a habitat favored by cowries, especially where a thin layer of sand overlays a hard substrate. In 1965, Schilder published a list of cowries according to their geographic distribution and noted the following species in the Gulf: *Cypraea carneola, C. caurica, C. felina fabula, C. gracilis, C. grayana, C. lentiginosa, C. pallida,* and *C. turdus*. Only *C. carneola, C. caurica, C. gracilis,* and *C. grayana* are found throughout both the Gulf and the Red Sea; *C. felina fabula, C. lentiginosa,*

Cuttlefish (*Sepia*) are often seen in shallow sandy areas and lagoons. (*Gunnar Bemert*)

and *C. pallida* are found in the Gulf but not in the Red Sea. A previously unreported species, *C. esontropia* was recently found feeding on sponges.

Manmade structures, usually connected with the oil industry, are numerous in the Saudi Arabian area of the Gulf, where ARAMCO has many offshore producing platforms as well as oil-well structures and port and navigational aids. Oysters of several kinds were found to be the main constituents of communities growing on these artificial structures, which were included with the hard-bottom biotopes in the ARAMCO study. Most important, both numerically and structurally, are those species that live with one valve permanently cemented to a support. There are several types, each with a seemingly different depth preference, but the most abundant from a depth of 10 meters to the bottom was the cockscomb oyster (tentatively identified as *Lopha cristagalli* and *Hyotissa hyotis*, which is a type having more angular folds forming tubular processes). *Spondylus exilis*, a large, thick-shelled, dome-shaped, thorny oyster with a straight aperture was only slightly less prevalent than the cockscomb, from a depth of 6 meters to the bottom. There are also large and small oysters (*Ostrea*) with sinuous apertures and jewel boxes (*Chama*), which were particularly firmly cemented. Sessile bivalves such as mussels (*Mytilus*) and pearl oysters (*Pinctada radiata* and *P. margaritifera*), were found on the platform legs between depths of 3 and 10 meters. Although

100

neither type of pearl oyster was particularly numerous on the platform, some individuals grew to exceptional sizes. One black-lipped oyster (*P. margaritifera*) found at 6 meters measured 22 centimeters in diameter. Very large individuals of the black bird oyster (*Pteria*) also occur in this depth range. Some gastropods were found on these artificial structures: a few top shells, wentletraps, and drupes, and a small number of nudibranchs.

THE OPEN SEA

Although many molluscs are truly pelagic or active swimmers, they are mostly deep-sea forms and are not found in the shallow waters of the Gulf.

The cuttlefish (*Sepia*) are capable of rapid and extensive swimming but remain close bound to a particular benthic community. The common octopus is not pelagic but benthic (that is, it swims only to escape danger). The same features that make the cephalopods biologically successful (high intelligence and tremendous mobility) have also made them extremely difficult to capture, so they have not yet been studied in the Gulf. They appear, however, to be abundant, though rather small (around 20 centimeters), and therefore probably belong to the worldwide genus *Loligo*, the coastal squids.

Glossary

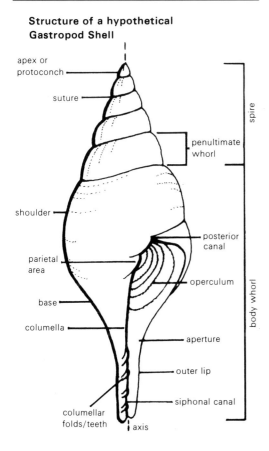

Structure of a hypothetical Gastropod Shell

apex or protoconch

suture

penultimate whorl

spire

shoulder

posterior canal

parietal area

operculum

base

body whorl

columella

aperture

outer lip

siphonal canal

columellar folds/teeth

axis

adductor muscle The single or double internal muscles by which the bivalve is attached inside its shell and which draw together the two portions to close it.

adductor scars Depressions marking the attachment of the muscles of the bivalve shell. Can be useful in identifying the species.

alga (pl. algae) A diverse group of plants ranging in size from microscopic phytoplankton to large seaweeds.

annelid A large group of worms, many of which are marine. Characterized by a body divided into a series of similar segments; the internal organs are also often segmented.

Aplacophora A class of little-known marine molluscs, also known as solenogasters.

aperture The opening at the last-formed margin of a gastropod snail shell from which the head and foot of the live animal may extend.

apex The earliest formed and highest part of a shell. It appears as the tip of the spire of a gastropod and generally consists of the embryonic shell. See protoconch.

aragonite A mineral composed of calcium carbonate but different from calcite in certain characteristics of crystallization and density; commonly, the innermost layers of a shell.

asymmetrical Not even or equal on both sides of an axis.

axis Imaginary line around which a spiral shell coils. The central structure in a spiral shell; also called a pillar.

base The end opposite the apex of the spire in snail shells.

beak The rounded or pointed part of a bivalve shell near or above the hinge, marking the point where growth of shell started. See umbo.

benthos Plants and animal inhabitants in or on the bottom of the sea.

biota The flora and fauna of a region.

biotope A uniform and defined area of the environment with a recognizable community of plants and animals for which it is the habitat.

Bivalvia The second largest class of molluscs. All are aquatic, both freshwater and marine species, and have two valves generally connected by an elastic ligament and closed by one adductor muscle (oysters) or by two (clams). There are, however, also some bivalved gastropods.

body whorl The last and usually largest whorl of a spiral univalve shell.

byssus A tuft of silky, long, fibrous threads that many bivalves secrete from their foot to anchor themselves to solid objects on the bottom.

calcareous Consisting of or containing calcium carbonate; of the nature of limestone.

calcite A mineral (calcium carbonate) crystallized in hexagonal form. See aragonite.

callus A thickened deposit of shelly material, especially around the aperture of a gastropod.

canal A groove or tube, such as that used for the siphon of a gastropod.

carnivorous Subsisting or feeding on animal tissues.

cephalic Pertaining to or toward the head.

Cephalopoda One of seven classes of mollusc. Some have external shells (*Nautilus*), and others have internal shells (cuttlefish and octopus). They are characterized by tentacles around a mouth, a highly developed nervous system, and eyes eimilar in complexity to those of vertebrates.

cerata Tuft-like projections on the backs of sea slugs, often used in respiration and for protection.

chiton A horny organic substance found in the ligament of bivalves, the operculum of some gastropods, and the internal shell of squids. A common name for a coat-of-mail shell. See Polyplacophora.

cilia Small hairlike projections on the surface of a cell or organ that beat rhythmically and cause movement of water or other fluids. Small larvae swim by beating cilia, and some adults, especially bivalves, use them to maintain the currents of moving water by which they eat and breathe.

class The primary divisions of a phylum. The Phylum Mollusca has seven classes, each of which includes a number of orders.

columella The central axis or axial pillar around which the whorls of a gastropod are coiled. A portion can be seen at the lower inner part of the aperture of most spiral univalves.

conchiolin Organic compound of protein of which the periostracum and the matrix of the limey parts of a shell are composed.

conchology The study of the hard parts of molluscs or shells. See malacology.

crenulated Delicately corrugated or finely wrinkled as seen on the edge of some bivalve shells or the outer lip of some snail shells. See *Terebra crenulata*.

dextral Gastropods in which the coiling is clockwise; said of a shell having the aperture on its right side when the apex is held upward; opposite of sinistral.

distal Away from the center of the body or point of attachment.

dorsal Relating to the back or upper side of an organism.

ecology A branch of science concerned with the inter-relationships between organisms and their environment.

ecosystem A natural unit that includes living and non-living parts interacting to produce a stable system (for example, a seashore).

endemic Prevalent or regularly found in a place.

environment The total physical, chemical, and biotic conditions surrounding an organism.

exoskeleton An external structure that supports the body, commonly called a shell.

family A grouping used in classification that includes a number of genera (for example, the Family Strombidae, which includes *Strombus* and *Lambis*).

fascia A broad, well-defined band of color; striped. See *Strombus fasciatus*.

fauna The animal life living in a given area or during a specified period of time, as opposed to flora, the plant life.

foot The muscular undersurface of the body of a mollusc on which it rests or moves; developed differently by unlike classes and species.

fossil Any hardened remains or traces of an organism preserved from past geologic times in the earth or rocks by natural causes.

fossa Shallow linear depression or cavity.

Gastropoda The class of molluscs that have a distinct head, a creeping foot, and a single, usually spirally coiled, asymmetrical shell (snails) but also including shell-less slugs and nudibranchs. They can live in the sea, in fresh water, or on land; herbivorous and carnivorous.

gastroverm See Monoplacophora.

genus (pl. genera) A grouping used in classification; a sub-division of a family including one to many species.

gill The organs used by most aquatic animals for breathing the air dissolved in water.

girdle The flexible leathery part of the mantle that encircles the shell plates of chitons and in which they are embedded.

gizzard A thickened, muscular stomach paved with calcareous plates designed for crushing food.

growth line Concentric lines parallel to a shell's margin, marking successive rest periods during growth and denoting former positions of the outer lip.

habitat The place where an organism lives.

herbivorous Feeding on plants or vegetable matter.

hermaphrodite An animal with both male and female reproductive organs that can produce both sperm and eggs.

holotype The single specimen designated as the type by the original author of the species, so designated at the time of the original description.

homonym Identical and independently proposed names for different species, genera, or taxa.

hydroids Marine invertebrates of the Phylum Coelenterata, one family being the fire corals (Milleporidae).

indigenous Native to the country.

intertidal zone The area between the low and high tide levels.

invertebrate Any animal without a backbone or vertebrae.

labial Pertaining to the lip or thickened edges of the gastropod's aperture.

Lamellibranchia See Pelecypoda or Bivalvia.

lamina(e) A thin plate or scale.

ligament A fibrous elastic band connecting the valves in bivalves and acting in opposition to the adductor muscles, (that is, causing the shell to gape when relaxed or severed).

lip See labial.

littoral The zone on the shore between high and low tide marks; belonging to, inhabiting, or taking place near the seashore.

maculate Patterned with blotches of rather large size. See *Terebra maculata*.

malacology The study of molluscs as soft animals. See conchology.

mantle A fleshy tunic or fold from the body wall of a mollusc that secretes the periostracum and shell (when present).

mantle cavity The space between the mollusc's body and its mantle which in bivalves and some gastropods forms the gill chamber.

Mollusca The second largest phylum in the animal kingdom. Invertebrates with a soft, unsegmented body and covered usually with a double or single shell or having an internal shell.

Monoplacophora Most primitive class of apparently partly segmented molluscs, thought to have been extinct but discovered alive in 1952.

nacre The pearly or iridescent layers of the interiors of some shells.

nekton Free-swimming aquatic animals (as squid).

nudibranch A type of gastropod slug, usually brilliantly coloured and having no shell.

omnivorous Eating both animal and vegetable foods.

operculum Horny or calcareous disc on the foot of a snail that can usually seal the shell's opening when the snail has retracted. The conches also use it for locomotion.

Opisthobranchia "Rear gills." One of three major subclasses of gastropods; includes most commonly the colorful nudibranchs, sea hares, and bubble shells.

order A grouping used in classification; includes a number of families and forms a subdivision of a class.

pallial line Fine single-line impression in a bivalve produced by the attachment of the mantle to the shell.

pallial sinus A notch or indentation in the pallial line of a bivalve that marks the position of retracted siphons.

paratype Those shell specimens, other than the holotype but collected at the same place and time, that were in front of the author when he was preparing the original description of a species.

parietal The inner wall of the aperture in a snail shell.

pearl A more or less spherical foreign object covered with layers of nacre by a mollusc.

pelagic Living in the surface waters of the open sea.

Pelecypoda A bivalve, "hatchet footed." The most obvious external feature is the possession of a shell consisting of two halves or valves hinged together at one edge.

penultimate Next-to-the-last formed; the last but one; the last whorl before the body whorl.

periostracum The skinlike outer organic layer(s) covering many shells; thick, brown and horny, hairy, or fibrous but sometimes thin and transparent like shellac.

phylum (pl. phyla) A chief division in the classification of the animal or plant kingdoms; the Phylum Mollusca, one of the divisions of the animal kingdom, is further divided into classes.

plankton Pelagic animals collectively as distinguished from coastal or bottom forms; a general name for the animal and plant life of the sea that floats in the water without purposeful swimming. Carried about by currents; a large percentage is microscopic.

Polyplacophora A class of molluscs known as chitons or coat-of-mail shells; characterized by eight symmetrical, overlapping, calcareous plates embedded in a girdle. Marine dwelling, they are found slowly creeping or clinging tightly to intertidal rocks (in most parts of the world), where they graze on algae.

proboscis Any long, flexible snout; the protruding feeding organ of a snail.

Prosobranchia Means "front gills." One of the three sub-classes of gastropods; includes the most common shelled snail-like shells.

protoconch The embryonic shell of a univalve formed during the larval stage of its life and present in the adult as the apical whorls and frequently clearly different from later whorls by a change of texture, color, or sculpture.

Pulmonata The most highly developed group of gastropods, often terrestial and air breathing.

radula The tonguelike organ possessed by most snails and all other molluscs except bivalves. Composed of a ribbon to which are fixed numerous toothlike projections often used as a rasp; variously developed by different classes and species.

Scaphopoda The simplest class of tusk-shelled molluscs.

serrate Notched or toothed at the edge like a saw.

sessile Permanently attached by the base, or sedentary, as are many benthic molluscs such as oysters. Opposite of vagile.

shell The protective (usually) covering of a mollusc secreted by its mantle. A hard, rigid, calcareous structure encasing a mollusc or covering some part of it with an outer organic layer.

sinistral Gastropods in which the coiling is counterclockwise; said of a snail having its aperture on the left side when the apex is held upward; opposite of dextral.

sinus A recess, indentation, or deeply cut cavity as in a shell.

siphon A fold or tube, usually formed from the mantle, through which a current of water passes. Found in carnivorous gastropods and many bivalves.

siphonal canal The tubular extension of the aperture.

slug Any snail with a greatly reduced shell or no shell at all.

snail A slow-moving gastropod having a protective and usually spiral shell.

species A group subordinate to a genus; having members that differ among themselves only in minor details of proportion, structure, or color.

spicules Small and often spiney processes on the girdle of a chiton.

spire The part of a spiral shell made up of all the whorls except the last and largest, or body whorl.

squamose Having scales.

stria (*pl. striae*) A narrow and shallow incised groove or line. See *Conus striatus*.

substrate An ecological term denoting the base on which an organism lives (for example, a sandy bottom of a subtidal environment).

suture The spiral line marking the junction of two whorls in a gastropod.

symmetrical Equal-sided, well balanced, having similar parts arranged in regular, reverse order on each side.

teeth The projections that form the hinge of a bivalve, which engage corresponding sockets in the opposite valves; also the chitinous plates on the radula.

tessellate Color patterns on the shell arranged in a checkerboard pattern or oblong patches.

torsion The embryological process in which the body of some gastropods is twisted within a few hours by rotating the parts of the larval mollusc behind the head 180° counterclockwise; independent of the process by which the shell is helically coiled in the form of a helicocone.

trochophore A ciliated larva typical of marine annelid worms but occurring in other invertebrate groups, including some of the molluscs.

tusk See Scaphopoda.

umbilicus A small, circular depression or indentation, commonly at the center of the base of the body whorl in some shells.

umbo The tip or very convex first-formed part of each valve of a bivalve.

univalve A molluscan snail of the class Gastropoda with only one piece of shell.

vagile Free moving. Opposite of sessile.

valves One of the separate parts or units making up the shell of a mollusc.

varix (*pl. varices*) A longitudinal, elevated ridge formed on the outer surface across the whorls of some molluscs by a thickened and reflected former lip during a resting phase of snail growth.

veliger A larval mollusc in the stage where it has a ciliated velum, or swimming membrane(s).

velum A piece of tissue, often in lobes and ciliated, used by veliger larva for locomotion and feeding.

ventral Toward the lower or bottom side away from the back; opposite the hinge in a bivalve.

visceral hump The section of a molluscan body never extended from the shell (when a shell is present).

whorl One complete spiral turn or coil of a spiral univalve shell.

zooxanthellae Microscopic, photosynthetic algae, symbiotic with giant clams (*Tridacna*) and reef-forming corals.

Bibliography

REFERENCE BOOKS AND
IDENTIFICATION GUIDES

ABBOTT, R. T. (editor). *Indo-Pacific Mollusca*. 3 volumes. Delaware Museum of Natural History, 1959–1976. An extremely complete reference with locality maps for the few families that have been covered.

ABBOTT, R. T. *Seashells of the World*. New York: Golden Press, 1962. The very best pocket reference for worldwide shelling.

ALLAN, J. *Australian Shells*. Melbourne: Georgian House, 1950.

ARNOLD, W. (compiler) A glossary of a thousand-and-one terms used in conchology: *The Veliger*, vol. 7 (supplement).

BOSS, K. J. Critical estimate of the number of recent mollusca: *Harvard University Occasional Papers on Mollusks*, vol. 3, no. 40, p. 88–111. The authoratative source on molluscan populations.

BURGESS, C. M. *The Living Cowries*. New York: Barnes, 1970. This classic cowrie reference has locality maps and clear photographs as well as descriptions of the characteristics of the living animals.

CERNOHORSKY, W. O. *Marine Shells of the Pacific*. 3 volumes. Sydney: Pacific Publications, 1978. A complete reference for any serious collector, although photographs of all species are not included.

DANCE, S. P. (editor) *The Collector's Encyclopaedia of Shells*. New York: McGraw Hill, 1974.

GEORGE, D. AND GEORGE, J. *Marine Life: An Illustrated Encyclopaedia of Invertebrates in the Sea*. London: Harrap, 1979.

HINTON, ALAN. *Shells of New Guinea and the Central Indo-Pacific*. Rutland: Tuttle, 1975.

HOUBRICK, R. S. The Family Cerithiidae in the Indo-Pacific: Monographs of Marine Mollusca, no. 1. Greenville, Delaware: American Malacologists, Inc., 1978.

LINDNER, G. *Field Guide to Seashells of the World*. New York: Van Nostrand Reinhold, 1978.

MARSH, J. A., AND RIPPINGALE, O. H. *Cone Shells of the World*. Brisbane: Jacarunda, 1968.

MORTON, J. E. *Molluscs*. London: Hutchinson, 1979. For the intermediate to advanced collector interested in biology.

NEWELL, P., AND NEWELL, P. *Seashells: A Naturalist's and Collector's Guide*. Oxford: Phaidon, 1979.

SCHILDER, F. A. The Geographical Distribution of Cowries: *The Veliger*, vol. 7, no. 3, p. 171–183.

SOLEM, A. *The Shell Makers: Introducing Molluscs*. New York: John Wiley, 1974.

THOMPSON, T. E. *Nudibranchs*. Hong Kong: T.F.H. Publications, 1976.

WAGNER, R. J. L., AND ABBOTT, R. T. *Van Nostrand's Standard Catalogue of Shells*. Princeton: Van Nostrand Company, 1967.

WALLS, J. G. *Cowries*. Hong Kong: T.F.H. Publications, 1975.

WALLS, J. G. *Cone Shells, A Synopsis of the Living Conidae*. Hong Kong: T.F.H. Publications, 1978.

WALLS, J. G. *Conchs, Tibias and Haros*. Hong Kong: T.F.H. Publications, 1980.

WILSON, B. R., AND GILLETT, K. *Australian Shells*. Rutland, Vt.: Tuttle, 1971.

YONGE, C. M., AND THOMPSON, T. E. *Living Marine Molluscs*. London: Collins, 1976.

ZEIGLER, R. F., AND PORRECA, H. C. *Olive Shells of the World*. Rochester Polychrome Press, 1969.

POPULAR BOOKS

ABBOTT, R. T. *Kingdom of the Seashell*. London: Hamlyn, 1973.

BOLMAN, J. *The Mystery of the Pearl*. Leiden: E. J. Brill, 1941.

COUSTEAU, J. Y., AND DIOLÉ, P. *Octopus and Squid: The Soft Intelligence*. London: Cassell, 1973.

FEININGER, A., AND EMERSON, W. *Shells*. London: Thames & Hudson, 1972.

KUNZ, G. F., AND STEVENSON, C. H. *The Book of the Pearl*. London: MacMillan, 1908.

PETRON, C., AND LOZET, J. B. *The Guinness Guide to Underwater Life*. London: Guinness Superlatives, 1975.

RITCHIE, C. *Shell Carving, History and Techniques*. London: Yoseloff, 1974.

SAUL, MARY. *Shells, An Illustrated Guide to a Timeless and Fascinating World*. Garden City, N.J.: Doubleday, 1974.

STIX, H., STIX, M., AND ABBOTT, R. T. *The Shell, 500 Million Years of Inspired Design*. New York: Harry Abrams, 1968.

RED SEA AND RED SEA MOLLUSCS

ANONYMOUS. *Red Sea and Gulf of Aden Pilot*. (11th edition). London: Hydrographer of the Navy, 1967. Corrected to February 6, 1971.

BEMERT, G., AND ORMOND, R. *Red Sea Coral Reefs*. London: Routledge and Kegan Paul, 1981.

FISHELSON, L. Ecology and distribution of the benthic fauna in the shallow waters of the Red Sea: *Marine Biology*, vol. 10, p. 113–133.

FOIN, T. C., AND RUEBUSH, L. P. Cypraeidae of the Red Sea at Massawa, Ethiopia, with a zoogeographical analysis based on the Schilders' regional lists: *The Veliger*, VOL. 12, p. 201–206.

FRICKE, H. W. *The Coral Seas*. New York: G. P. Putnam's Sons, 1973.

HAM, C. L. Jeddah check list—Cowries: *Journal of the Saudi Arabian Natural History Society*, vol. 1, no. 2, p. 10–14.

HUGHES, R. N. Biota of reef flats and limestone cliffs near Jeddah, Saudi Arabia: *Journal of Natural History*, vol. 11, p. 77–96.

ISSEL, ARTURO. *Malacologia del Mar Rosso*. Pisa: Editori della Biblioteca Malacologica, 1869.

O'MALLEY, J. Cowries of the Jeddah–Red Sea area identification guide: *Of Sea and Shore* (undated supplement).

ORMOND, R. Conserving the Red Sea: *Journal of the Saudi Arabian Natural History Society*, vol. 6, no. 18, p. 8–11.

ORMOND, R. Requirements and Progress in Marine Conservation in the Red Sea: *Progress in Underwater Science*, vol. 3, p. 165–176.

ROESSLER, C. *Underwater Wilderness, Life at the Great Reefs*. New York: Chanticleer Press, undated.

SKIPWITH, P. *The Red Sea and Coastal Plain of the Kingdom of Saudi Arabia, Technical Record TR-1973-1*. Jeddah, Saudi Arabian Directorate General of Mineral Resources, 1973.

ARABIAN GULF AND GULF MOLLUSCS

ANONYMOUS. *Persian Gulf Pilot.* (11th edition). London: Hydrographer of the Navy, 1967. Corrected to 1980.

BASSON, P. W., BURCHARD, J. E., HARDY, J. T., AND PRICE, A. R. G. *Biotopes of the Western Arabian Gulf.* Dhahran: ARAMCO Department of Loss Prevention and Environmental Affairs, 1977.

BIGGS, H. E. J., AND GRANTIER, L. L. A preliminary list of the marine Mollusca of Ras Tanura, Persian Gulf: *Journal of Conchology*, vol. 24, no. 11, p. 387–392.

SMYTHE, K. R. The marine Mollusca of the U.A.E., Arabian Gulf: *Journal of Conchology*, vol. 30, no. 1, p. 57–80.

SMYTHE, K. R. The Tornatinidae and Retusidae of the Arabian Gulf: *Journal of Conchology*, vol. 30, no. 2, p. 93–98.

SAUDI ARABIA

ANONYMOUS. *An Introducteon to Saudi Arabian Antiquities.* Riyadh: Department of Antiquities and Museums, Ministry of Education, 1975.

ANONYMOUS. *The Times World Atlas* (Comprehensive edition). London: Times Books Ltd., 1980.

AZZI, R. *Saudi Arabian Portfolio.* Zug, Switzerland: First Azimuth, 1978.

BINDAGJI, H. H. *Atlas of Saudi Arabia.* Oxford: Oxford University Press, 1980.

AL FARSI, F. *Saudi Arabia, A Case Study in Development.* London: Stacey International, 1978.

NYROP, R. F., BENDERLY, CARTER, EGLIN, AND KIRCHNER. *Area Handbook for Saudi Arabia.* Washington, D.C.: U.S. Government Printing Office, 1971.

PESCE, A. *Jeddah: Portrait of an Arabian City.* Naples: Falcon Press, 1974.

ROSS, H. C. *Bedouin Jewellery in Saudi Arabia.* London: Stacey International, 1978.

VINCETT, B. A. L. *Wild Flowers of Central Saudi Arabia.* Milano: printed by Garzanti, 1979.

Index